Rare Breeds

Ralph Whitlock

RARE
BREEDS

The vulnerable survivors

Prism Press

Title page illustration of Jacob sheep by Sally Anne Thompson

Published in 1980 by
PRISM PRESS
Stable Court
Chalmington
Dorchester
Dorset DT2 0HB

Designed by Alphabet and Image Ltd
Sherborne, Dorset

ISBN 0 904727 87 4

Printed in Great Britain by Henry Ling Limited, Dorset Press, Dorchester

Contents

Acknowledgements

The publishers would like to thank the following for supplying photographs: Agricultural Institute, Co. Galway, pages 65 top, 67, 76 bottom, 82 top; T. Ash, West Wales Farm Park, 21, 88-9, 95, 146; Edward Ashpole, 26 top; Reidar Bogat, 55 bottom; British Farmer & Stockbreeder, 97, 98, 100, 105 top; British Wool Marketing Board, 62, 64, 68, 69, 72, 73, 74-5, 80, 84, 87, 88, 90; Bundesminsterium Fuer Land und Forstwirtschaft, 31 top; Ian Cameron, 79; W. W. Christie, 53; Dartmoor Sheep Association, 66; Farmers' Weekly, 151 top, 155; The Field, 17 top right, 24, 25, 28 top, 42, 59, 60, 61, 78, 85, 99, 108 right, 113, 123 top; Finnish Ministry of Agriculture, 40 top right, 47 top; J. Gibbs-Smith, 37; The Gloucester Cattle Society, 43; Italian Ministry of Agriculture, 38 right, top and bottom, 39, 44 top; Lleyn Sheep Society, 75; Ministerie van Landbouw en Visserij, 32 top, 36; Ministro do Agricultura, Madrid, 18 bottom, 19 top, 27, 45, 49 top, 51 bottom; Munchener Tierpark,16; Museum of English Rural Life, Reading, 9, 10, 12, 35, 47 bottom, 94, 101, 102, 104; National Pig Breeders' Association, 96, 103; National Sheep Association, 65 bottom, 71, 81, 82 bottom, 83; Northern Dairy Shorthorn Society, 41; Poultry World, 109 top, 127 top, 143; A. Rice, 108 left, 109 bottom, 110-12, 114-17, 118 right, 119, 120, 121 right, 122 top, 123 bottom, 124-6, 127 bottom, 128-42, 144-5, 147, 149-50, 151 bottom, 152-4, 156; M. H. Rosenberg, 91; Rothamsted Collection, 11; Salers Herd Society, 52 top; Brian Spooner, 77, 86, 93; Société Centrale d'Aviculture de France, 118 top left, 121 left, 122 bottom; Statens Landruk-information, 54; Philip Street, 15 bottom; Flora Stuart, 20, 52 bottom; Swiss Cattle Breeders' Federation, 30 bottom, 33; A. L. Tanner, 28 bottom; Tarentaise Herd Society, 55 top; Sally Anne Thompson, 2-3, 70; Ulster Folk and Transport Museum, 34, 105 bottom; University of Oklahoma Press, 17 bottom, 18 top, 23, 24 top, 26 bottom, 29, 30 top, 31 bottom, 32 bottom, 38 left, 40 left, 40 bottom right, 44 bottom, 46, 48, 49 bottom, 50, 51 top, 56, 58 top; Whitebred Shorthorn Association, 58; Ralph Whitlock, 76 top; Agnes Winter, 89.

This book contains many old and historic photographs, some of which are reproduced here for the first time. Inevitably the standard of photography is not what we would expect of modern photographic techniques. However this book remains the most comprehensive pictorial listing of rare breeds of farm animals yet published.

Introduction

The realization that many species of mammals, birds and other forms of wild life are in danger of extinction has become widespread only in the second half of the present century. Until quite recently sportsmen in pursuit of trophies continued to shoot tigers, hunt oryx and slaughter the big game of Africa without a thought for the future. Then, quite suddenly, came the appreciation of the fact that, unless a new attitude quickly prevailed, hundreds of species would soon be following the great auk and the dodo along the path to oblivion. This enlightenment has been accompanied by a new criterion that a threatened species is worth preserving in its own right, regardless of its utilitarian or aesthetic value. We now protect such unattractive creatures as crocodiles, simply because we recognize their right to their place in the ecology of their habitat.

To arouse interest in the survival of rare breeds of domesticated animals has taken even longer. Until very recently they have been, at the best, museum specimens — examples of experiments that have outlived their usefulness. A breed, after all, is man-made. It is a race of creatures evolved by man for his own purposes. So long as those purposes retain their importance, and so long as the breed in question continues to fulfil them, all is well. But let the purposes become obsolete or the breed become superseded by something more efficient, and the incentive to preserve the breed is lost. What man has made he can also destroy or allow to perish through neglect.

A breed is not a species but corresponds to a race or variety in nature. By natural selection species are continually adapting themselves to changing environments. The individuals which best adapt themselves are those which survive and therefore produce the next generation. For example, a land mammal with a wide distribution in Africa may develop, within that vast continent, a number of distinct races, as local populations adapt to local conditions such as desert, mountain, savannah or jungle. Yet the races thus evolving will still belong to the same species; they will interbreed if brought together.

The process is most easily observed in species which multiply rapidly. As we know only too well, various disease micro-organisms can quickly evolve races immune to the antibiotics with which we strive to control them. A few years ago rats began to develop a race resistant to the poisons commonly used against them. After the mid-1950s a decimated rabbit population in Australia, Britain and much of Europe survived the onslaught of myxomatosis by developing a similar immunity.

A breed may be defined as a man-manipulated race. Instead of leaving evolution to nature, man takes a hand and decides which individuals shall survive to become the parents of the next generation.

In the process he first formulates, or should formulate, a clear idea of the characteristics he wants to develop in the species in which he is interested. Then he selects for breeding those individuals which possess those qualities, discarding all others. After several generations of such selection, the stock 'breeds true' and the breed is established.

The fantastic results which can be achieved by the process are illustrated by the parade at a dog show. Boxers, bloodhounds, Pekinese, chihuahuas, bulldogs, collies, setters and Yorkshire terriers are all dogs, and they recognise each other as such. The mating of two springer spaniels will produce more springer spaniels. The mating of a springer spaniel with, say, a bull terrier will produce a lively litter of mongrel puppies.

The continuance of a breed therefore depends on the continuance of controlled mating. So long as a sufficient number of breeders is interested in maintaining the breed, the breed flourishes. When interest flags, the breed becomes rare and may vanish.

Attempting to define a rare breed is a precarious task. It is important not to omit from the list any primitive genetical material which could conceivably be in danger, even though it may seem safe at the moment. On the other hand, the application of the adjective 'rare' to a breed often seems little short of defamation to dedicated breeders.

It is an unfortunate fact that danger can creep up unawares. Many a time I have heard the argument, 'How can you call this breed rare? Why, from my window I can see more than a hundred of them, and I know for a fact that there are at least as many again within a ten-mile radius.' The comment could well have been applied to Longhorn cattle in the early 1960s, but when, within a few weeks of the death of the biggest breeder, his herd of about 150 was slaughtered, the breed was certainly for a time in peril. In the early 1950s the Shropshire breed of sheep, with their long and distinguished history, led the classes at the big agricultural shows in the west midlands and seemed to have an assured future. Yet by 1975 they were down to less than 500 ewes. The story of the Wiltshire Horn breed of sheep, which, early in the nineteenth century, dropped from more than half-a-million to only a few small flocks in the space of thirty or forty years and were then only just saved from extinction, is a salutary example of what can happen.

The fact that a breed may be relatively abundant locally but rare elsewhere has to be reckoned with. It has a bearing, too, on breeds that are now being introduced to countries other than their homeland. Many of them represent types of considerable antiquity and therefore presumably possessing a reservoir of primitive genes. Within their provincial limits they are not uncommon; elsewhere, they are.

Small numbers of them have within the past ten or fifteen years been introduced to Britain and America. I asked a prominent agriculturist with a foothold in both countries whether he would expect to find, in a publication dealing with rare breeds, something about, for instance, the Tarentaise or the Marchigiana. When I had explained to him that they are breeds of cattle (for the names meant nothing to him) he replied, 'Sure. They're rare, aren't they?' When I put the same question to a breeder of one of them he was affronted by the very suggestion. Both breeds, like many others, are at present reasonably plentiful in the provinces where they originate but are little known elsewhere.

At present . . . but could they ever become rare? Probably the greatest threat lies in their native land. The Irish breeds of cattle and sheep have become rare and in some instances extinct not through slaughter or neglect but through 'improvement'. They have been crossed with and graded up by imported stock till they have been altered out of recognition, their ancient heredity submerged and almost lost. In some countries, such as Norway, grading up to achieve uniformity is official policy, which spells doom to the older, more primitive, less productive types. It could happen almost anywhere. 'It seems a good idea to preserve the genetic variation that exists, so that at any time in the future we can go back to it.' Once let the improvers get at the provincial breeds of Europe and they may become rare more quickly than at present seems possible.

When we study the changing fortunes of a breed, therefore, we become involved in a study of human motives. Why do men take such trouble to establish a breed and then lose interest in it?

Seeking examples again in the realm of dogs, we see that the breeds were originally developed for specific utilitarian purposes. Wolfhounds were bred for hunting wolves; foxhounds for hunting foxes; terriers for digging out foxes which had gone to ground; sheep-dogs for rounding up sheep; retrievers for retrieving game. The massive forequarters and squat nose of the bulldog fitted him for bull-baiting in the bad old days. Pekinese are alleged to have been bred for Chinese emperors whose emblem was the lion and who insisted on being accompanied, in the absence of lions, by small lion-like dogs.

Foxhounds, terriers and retrievers still engage in their accustomed tasks, but bulldogs and Pekinese have outlived their original purposes in life. No one baits bulls with dogs nowadays, and there are no Chinese emperors. Logically these breeds should therefore have become extinct, but they have been preserved by fanciers, who admire them and compete with each other at shows.

When utility ceases to have a value, exaggerated standards often take over. The cages at a pigeon show will illustrate the absurd lengths to which fanciers are prepared to go. Here we can see pigeons with feathers on their toes longer than those on their wings, pigeons which lean over backwards to avoid their deformed chests and have never seen their own feet, pigeons with snub beaks so short that they can hardly peck their own food. Show points which were once of mild interest have, in the absence of any utilitarian purpose in breeding the stock, become supreme. To all but the dedicated breeders the results are ridiculous, and the birds themselves must in many instances live lives of discomfort.

For a time the early breeders of commercial farm livestock fell into the same snare. Once they had discovered what they could do by judicious selection of breeding stock they pushed things to extremes.

Much of the earliest recognised work in scientific livestock breeding began in England with Robert Bakewell, who flourished at Dishley, in Leicestershire, in the 1770s and 1780s. It is now appreciated that he did not work in a vacuum but borrowed many of his ideas from a Mr Webster, who built up a formidable reputation as a cattle-breeder in the same neighbourhood when Bakewell was a youth. However, Bakewell was undoubtedly one of the first to adopt an intelligent and consistent policy of breeding for pre-selected characteristics. His chosen cattle were English Longhorns. He also worked with Teeswater sheep and Large White pigs.

A little later the Collings brothers, Robert and Charles, began a similar programme with Shorthorn cattle. In 1784 they selected an outstanding local bull, Hubback, on whom they founded an improved Shorthorn breed. Fifty years later a noted Shorthorn breeder testified that 'we have no superior shorthorns which do not claim descent . . . from Hubback.'

Hubback belonged to the old Teeswater type of cattle, indigenous to County Durham, England, which also produced the Blackwell Ox (Blackwell being a village in that county). And although we do not have a portrait of Hubback, we do possess one of the Blackwell Ox. A line engraving, by one J. Bailey from a painting by George Cuit, it is one of the earliest prints of cattle in existence. Dated 1780, it portrays an animal which was slaughtered, at the age of six years, in 1779. It therefore belongs to the first recognised period of cattle improvement and can give us some idea of what the old domestic stock of England was like before the improvers got at it.

It is not a bad animal. A bit heavy on the forequarters and somewhat short in the body but, on the whole, quite well-proportioned. There is none of the gross obesity so evident in cattle of twenty or thirty years later. One has the feeling that George Cuit painted it from life. It does look like a real ox.

The Blackwell Ox

The Durham Ox. Etching, 1802.

Thereafter, unreality begins to creep in. It starts with the Durham Ox, of which there is an etching dated 1802. This celebrated, or notorious, animal, bred by Charles Colling, spent six years touring Britain and displaying, at shows and similar fiestas, its 27 hundredweights of flesh and bone to fascinated audiences. At the time of the portrait it stood 5½ feet high at the shoulder, was 11 feet long and measured just over 5 feet across the middle of the back.

The picture shows the Durham Ox in a conventional posture, full side on and legs perfectly positioned. The body is roughly rectangular, though over-fat and with a pendulous dewlap. Although this animal is very different from the Blackwell Ox, one feels that the picture probably portrays it as it really was. Breeders had evidently been working for a deep, massive body and had been so successful that the head appears small and the legs short in proportion.

Once these qualities became popular, breeders pushed them to extremities. Size of body was everything, heads and legs being merely secondary though unfortunately essential appendages. The vogue took such a hold that breeders who could afford to pay to have portraits of their animals painted insisted that the ideal for which they were aiming should be depicted on canvas, even if the actual beasts fell short of perfection. In some instances, where the actual measurements are recorded, we can check the accuracy of the pictures and so establish the extent of the distortion.

With pigs the craze was pushed to even greater lengths. The Yorkshire Hog, known to us from an engraving by R Pollard, is rightly termed a 'stupendous creature'. At the age of four years it weighed 1,344 pounds, stood 12½ hands high and was nearly 10 feet long. In the picture it looks as though it could easily swallow its attendant, Joseph Hudson, who eyes it as warily as an animal trainer approaching a particularly short-tempered tiger. 'He would feed to a greater weight were he not raised up so often to exhibit his stature', says a contemporary caption. Other pigs, which

10

The Yorkshire Hog. Aquatint by R. Pollard, 1809.

were not called upon to display themselves so frequently, became so heavy that they were unable to stand up without the aid of props.

The ideals thus portrayed were, of course, unworthy. The breeders were demanding size, weight and flesh at the expense of what we now consider more admirable qualities. We may perhaps put it down to the natural exuberance of men who had just discovered what could be done by the new technique of controlled breeding.

The extravagances of the early improvers did the Shorthorn breed, to which most of them were confined, no good at all. In protest against the exaggerated beef qualities the breed split into two camps, one concentrating on a dairy or dual-purpose animal while the other remained faithful to the beef concept. For more than a century the two types existed side by side and dominated much of the cattle scene throughout the British Isles. The beef type in particular, its grossness refined, was also exported to the U.S.A., Australia,

South America, New Zealand, Canada and many other countries and played a prominent part in the development of their beef industry. But in Britain so much indiscriminate crossing occurred at the non-pedigree levels that buyers were never sure of what they were purchasing in the open market. While knowledgeable breeders maintained high standards in their own herds, ordinary farmers tended to buy breeding stock in markets by looks alone. Because of beef stock in her ancestry a fine-looking Shorthorn heifer would often prove a disappointing producer of milk. When, in the 1920s, Friesian cattle became more readily available in Britain, they quickly usurped the Dairy Shorthorn position not so much by reason of their heavier yields as by the greater consistency of their performance. Both in the beef and dairy sectors Shorthorns have fallen behind some of their specialist rivals, though the surviving pure-bred herds have now eliminated the old reproach.

The fortunes of the Shorthorns thus illustrate the pitfalls that can encompass a popular

Bakewell's Leicester sheep. Coloured lithograph, c. 1850.

breed. It is not without significance that most of the breeds with which the early improvers worked have gone into eclipse. Robert Bakewell's Longhorns have, from being the common cattle type of Midland England, become a rare breed; and few flocks survive of his Leicester sheep.

If it is true that breeds become rare through competition with better, it may be argued that the casualties should be allowed to slip into limbo. However, men, who are responsible for fashioning breeds, have made mistakes in the past and may do so again. The development of the very qualities which enable the new-comers to triumph may presently reveal hidden weaknesses. Breeds are all the more vulnerable today because of the prevalence of artificial insemination, whereby a popular cattle sire, for instance, may father scores of thousands of calves. Any flaws he may possess will make a proportional impact on the breed.

In the search for higher and more efficient production, better conversion rates, early maturity and other qualities on which modern livestock production is based, the risk is inherent of sacrificing hardihood, resistance to diseases, good mothering qualities and other intangible characteristics. Often realization of the danger does not come until quite late in the programme. Safety lies in the existence of a genetical reservoir of primitive material from which supplies may be drawn to correct errors.

Commenting on an allied project, to establish the first semen bank in England, Dr Kevin O'Connor, of the English Milk Marketing Board, stated at its inception:

All breeds of cattle are changing all the time, and it seems a good idea to preserve the genetic variation that exists, so that at any time in the future we can go back to it. Thirty years ago many of our beef breeds had a lot more size; then many of them

12

were bred smaller and neater; now we are trying to get the size back into them again. It might have saved us a lot of time today if we had been able to go to the store and get some semen from a big, rough Hereford of the early 1900s.

Breeds tend to flourish only for as long as they have breed societies sufficiently strong to stage competitive classes at agricultural shows. When they decline past that point they are kept alive for a time by a few enthusiasts, in the hope of a better day. In the end, discouragement can result in their complete disappearance. In some instances they linger on even when no nucleus of breeders is interested in their support. When in the early 1960s I acquired, at a public auction, an odd lot of about twenty Jacob sheep I tried in vain, through articles and letters in the Press, to find anyone else who might be interested in forming a breed society to help in the preservation of the breed. My efforts were evidently a little premature, for the existing breed society, formed in 1969, now has more than 150 registered flocks containing in all over 3,000 sheep.

Here, however, we have a primitive type rather than a breed. Before ever Bakewell and his contemporaries started their pioneering work there existed primitive types of livestock which had evolved through the centuries. These represented the basic material on which the improvers worked.

No doubt through the unrecorded years there were individual breeders who appreciated the value of a good ram or a good bull. Long ago in ancient India a king decreed that in each locality in his domain a committee of farmers and cattle-breeders should be set up to inspect all bull calves offered to the priest. The best were to be reserved for use as sires. When fully grown they were turned loose to enable them to mate with any village cows. By this method the wise king argued that the standard of livestock in his kingdom would be steadily improved. It was not his fault that later his committees became corrupt and accepted bull calves of low grades.

In general, however, natural selection rather than human control shaped the development of the early types of livestock. A sheep farmer of Cumberland, England, once assured me that he always bred his own stock. No sheep brought in from other districts would thrive on his mountain. The reason was that, over the generations, his home-bred sheep had become acclimatised to their environment. Not only were they innured to the austere climate but they had arrived at a compromise with all the parasites and diseases that infested the mountain pastures. They had developed, if not an immunity, at least a formidable resistance to familiar ills. The natural process of the survival of the fittest was operating.

So, in the study of and search for rare breeds, it is not only man-made breeds which attract our interest. Beyond them are the original stock from which modern breeds were developed. They are termed breeds for want of a better word, and for many of them breed societies have now been formed. But in reality they are races or varieties which have, to a large extent, evolved naturally and for that reason are remarkably well adapted to their environment.

Until the past two hundred years there was little specialization in the breeding of farm livestock. Cattle were expected to pull a plough and a cart, to rear calves, to provide milk (chiefly for butter and cheese), and finally to produce a meaty carcase. Sheep were, in the first instance, valued primarily for their milk, but always with wool and meat as important secondary products. One of the earliest uses for poultry was for cock-fighting. Pigs were essentially scavengers. For all farm animals life was hard, and only the hardiest of them could survive. The qualities fostered by the grim conditions may now be of the utmost value in reinforcing the genetic inheritance of modern breeds rendered soft or vulnerable by excessive specialization.

Breed societies are, for the most part, a product of the nineteenth and twentieth centuries. They exist to promote the interests of the breed, an operation which involves ensuring that the highest standards are maintained. They normally keep pedigree herd or flock books, in which every pure-bred animal accepted by the society is entered.

A breed society devoted to the maintenance and survival of a rare breed otherwise threatened with extinction is a phenomenon of the past two decades. One of the earliest was the Texas Longhorn Breeders' Association, formed in Texas in 1964. We have already noted the Jacob Sheep Breeders' Society, formed in England in 1969.

In 1968 a movement started in England to form an organization for the preservation of all rare breeds of British livestock. In August of that year the Royal Agricultural Society of England and the Zoological Society of London set up a Working Party to study the project. Two years later two university students carried out a survey of British breeds thought to be in danger. The results were discussed at a conference held at the National Agricultural Centre, Warwickshire, England, in the autumn of 1971, when it was decided to recommend the formation of a Trust. This, the Rare Breeds Survival Trust, was formally set up on 13 January 1972, with headquarters at the National Agricultural Centre.

Shortly afterwards several groups of cattle and sheep were transferred from the grounds of the Zoological Society at Whipsnade to the National Agricultural Centre, and some were moved on to a farm park established at Guiting Power, in England's Cotswold country, by Mr J. L. Henson, chairman of the Trust. Visiting the park soon after its establishment I found the biggest concentration of rare breeds in Britain, comprising the following: Old Gloucestershire, White Park, Dexter, Longhorn and West Highland cattle, and Soay, Orkney, Moorit Shetland, Improved Shetland, Manx Loghtan, White-faced Woodland, Jacob, Cotswold, St Kilda, Portland, Norfolk Horn and Lincoln Longwool sheep.

Incidentally, the practical problems of keeping such a collection are not as formidable as might be imagined. It is not necessary to keep each breed in a separate enclosure all the year. All the sheep run together except for a few weeks at mating time, as do most of the female cattle. Special precautions are needed only for the adult males.

Since then many more collections have been formed on farms and estates and other breed societies have been started. Exhibits of rare breeds have appeared at many agricultural shows, and the Trust itself now organises an annual show and sale. A semen bank for rare breeds of cattle has been established. In the Orkney Islands a colony of the rare North Ronaldshay sheep, which live mainly on seaweed gathered from the shore, is flourishing and, closely studied, is providing much valuable ecological information. The Trust runs a very lively monthly magazine, *The Ark*, edited by the secretary at The Ark, Winkleigh, Devon, England.

Something of international significance was started by the formation of the Trust in Their interest aroused, other countries are forming their own similar organizations. The Rare Breeds Trust of the Netherlands was founded in February 1976. Early in 1977 a society, the Ouessant Sheep Breeders' Group, was formed in France to preserve the Ouessant breed of sheep, reputed to be the smallest in the world. A recent survey has shown about thirty breeds of sheep in danger of extinction in Bulgaria, as a result of which the Bulgarian Government is providing a subsidy to preserve them and improve their status. Private individuals are establishing their own collections in Germany. Meantime, the British Trust is continually widening its interests, which now include horses, pigs, goats, poultry, geese and, to a limited extent, rabbits, as well as cattle and sheep.

In much of Africa, Asia and South America the situation is as it was in Europe and North America before modern techniques of controlled breeding were employed. The types of livestock found in those countries are not usually the most productive, from a western point of view, but they are often triumphs of adaptation to difficult environmental conditions. The genes they have developed through centuries of struggle could be invaluable to breeders of the future. These breeds are eminently worthy of study, and we shall allow them to founder to our immense loss.

Cattle

Introduction

There is general agreement that European cattle have their origins in two primitive types or species, *Bos primigenius* (the Aurochs), and *Bos longifrons* (the so-called *Celtic shorthorn*). Modern authorities suspect that *Bos longifrons* may not be a separate species but may, in fact, be a degenerate type of *Bos primigenius*, reduced in size and refined in bone structure by long domestication.

Wall painting of black bull, 15,000–10,000 B.C. Lascaux, France.

The aurochs was a large, fierce, forest beast that roamed over Europe, Asia and North Africa in prehistoric times, finally becoming extinct in the seventeenth century (the last died in Poland in 1627). In the present century it has been reconstructed by an imaginative genetic process by Heinz and Lutz Heck. The new aurochs, which can be seen in several central European zoos, is a mighty and impressive animal, though not quite attaining the reputed dimensions of the original bull which, according to Caesar, stood more than 6 feet high at the shoulders. It carried and carries a great pair of horns. *Bos longifrons*, by contrast, was a small delicately boned animal, perhaps no larger than the modern Dexter, with short, curved horns and a long, narrow face.

In addition to these two types, the Indian zebu has contributed characteristics to a number of modern breeds, notably in Africa, southern Europe and America, as well as in Asia. The most conspicuous zebu features

Present-day aurochs

Bos primigenius, the aurochs.

thus transmitted are the shoulder hump and pendulous dewlap and sheath.

The domestication of cattle probably occurred during the nomadic stage of Man's career. Each civilization as it becomes illuminated by the light of archaeology appears to possess cattle. The prime purpose for which the animals were first subdued and valued is speculative, but early representations of cattle show them being milked, suckling calves, being involved in religious ceremonies and participating in sport. The use of cattle for traction probably came later. At an early date cattle were doubtless regarded as visible symbols of wealth and served as a kind of currency.

The coloration of primitive cattle is a subject that has aroused some controversy. It has been widely held that piebald and skewbald animals denote controlled breeding and therefore domestication. However, rock paintings of hunting scenes of about 3000 BC from the Tassili Plateau in the central Sahara depict many such specimens, all bearing long, sickle-shaped horns. The Lascaux caves of southwestern France, too, dating from 20,000 or 30,000 BC, depict animals with white as a basic body colour, though in many instances peppered or splotched with red or black and usually with head and neck of some dark colour. Pictures of the bulls employed in the arenas of Minoan Crete also show a dappled red-and-white pattern, though these animals were almost certainly either domesticated or feral.

Undoubtedly one of the oldest colour features, which has the same protective significance as the white scut of a rabbit or deer, is the white dorsal stripe and tail, technically known as 'finching'. Modern examples of this ancient hallmark are the Old Gloucestershire, the Pinzgau and, of course, the Hereford.

Alderney

Old English records are liable to cause some confusion because they often refer to imported cattle from the Channel Islands indiscriminately as Guernseys, Jerseys or Alderneys. It seems, however, that in the course of the centuries the race of cattle on the island of Alderney did develop into a type distinct from the Guernsey, though much nearer to that than to the Jersey, at least in colour. A painting of 'An Alderney Cow' by the artist J. R. Ward, R.A., in 1828 shows a rather small, short-bodied animal with pronounced white markings but of Guernsey type. It is suggested that the basic stock may have belonged to the now rare French breed, Froment du Leon, with possibly some Norman blood, and there seems to have been some introduction of Dutch cattle to Guernsey and possibly Alderney in the later Middle Ages.

Present status

Almost certainly extinct, owing to the entire stock of Alderney cattle having been moved to Guernsey during the second world war and there merged with Guernsey cattle. But it may have died out before then.

Description

Conflicting evidence. In spite of Ward's painting, later accounts (1892 and 1918) describe the Alderney as 'larger and darker in colour than the Jersey but otherwise similar in appearance'. But it is also said that cattle from Jersey, Guernsey and even France were sometimes taken to Alderney before being shipped to England and were therefore called 'Alderneys' when they arrived.

Uses

Originally, no doubt, bred for work as well as for milk but latterly a dairy breed.

Alentejana

An indigenous breed in southern Portugal.

Present status

Widespread but may decline in competition with other more advanced breeds.

Description

A large, coarse animal. Colour, reddish brown with a few white markings. Horns, long, wide spreading and curved backwards. Bulls weigh 1600 to 1800 pounds; cows 1000 to 1200 pounds. Light on the hindquarters.

Uses

All-purpose though primarily for draught. Said to be a poor milker. Undeveloped so far.

Angler, or ANGELN ───────

An ancient breed living in Schleswig — Holstein and originally in adjacent parts of Denmark.

Present status

Uncommon but not thought to be in any immediate danger.

Description

A dark red breed, of medium size. Weight up to 2200 pounds in bulls, 1300–1400 pounds in cows. Short horns, curving forward a little in the females.

Uses

Primarily a dairy breed, though as a compact, well-fleshed animal it has some beef potential. Average lactation yields just short of 10,000 pounds of milk, with high butterfat content. Has contributed very extensively to the development of the Danish Red and also to some of the dairy breeds of eastern Europe.

Asturiana ───────────────

An indigenous breed of Asturias, in northern Spain.

Present status

Widespread in its native province but could quickly decline in competition with more productive breeds.

Description

The breed is split into two not-very-distinct types, the Mountain Asturiana being of a darker red colour than the light red Valley animals. Horns, medium, curved upwards and outwards. Bulls weigh up to 1800 pounds, cows, 1100 to 1300 pounds; according to feeding and locality, the Valley Asturiana tending to be heavier than the Mountain.

Uses

All-purpose, with a traditional emphasis on draught. Little developed so far.

Barrendas Espanolas

The indigenous breed of the south-western corner of Spain.

Present status

Probably satisfactory.

Description

Unlike the other Spanish breeds, this is a white breed, spotted or blotched with black or red. Horns, medium, curving outwards and then forward and upward. Bulls weigh up to 1800 pounds; cows to 1400 pounds.

Uses

Originally a draught animal, but its beef potential is now being developed to some extent.

Belted Galloway

Belted or "sheeted" cattle are found in many parts of the world. Lord David Stuart, who investigated their origins and published the results in his book *An Illustrated History of Belted Cattle* (1970) traced existing herds or individuals in mixed herds in Switzerland, Austria, southern Germany, Italy, Yugo-Slavia, Poland, Holland (see Lakenvelders), U.S.A. and Mongolia, with probable domiciles in a number of other countries. See also the Belted Welsh Black cattle.

In the Scottish lowlands and the English border counties it seems that from time immemorial there has been a sprinkling of Belties among Galloway cattle. Lord David Stuart quotes Mr Percy Laidlaw, a noted Galloway breeder, who in 1944 wrote:

> In the days before the railways, when cattle were driven from Galloway and Dumfries to Norfolk Fairs, the drovers always liked to have a beltie amongst the bunch, so that in the dark days they could pick out the way the cattle were heading ... As you will know, it has been quite common amongst the purest bred blacks to have a belted calf now and again.

Mr Laidlaw thought that the prejudice that developed against Belties was due to the belief that the coloration denoted a crossing with the Ayrshire. When the Galloway Cattle Society was formed in 1877 it was decided to admit only black cattle. The Belties had had their champions, however, notably a Lady Melville who, in the early years of the nineteenth century, introduced them to her husband's estate at Haltwhistle, Northumberland, and encouraged the tenants and neighbours to use her Beltie bulls. In spite of the

official ban on the Belties, ample survived for a breed society to be started, specifically for them, in 1921.

Present status

Although rare, the Belted Galloway is by no means a threatened breed. Lord David Stuart's survey listed four foundation herds and one other surviving at the end of the second world war. Since then a number of new herds has been formed, particularly south of the border, where the recognition is growing that, in addition to its commercial qualities, the Beltie is an attractive animal to have roaming in a park.

Since the war a thriving export trade has developed. The United States now has its own American Belted Galloway Cattle Breeders' Association, formed in 1951, which caters for breeders from Florida to Quebec (Canada). Some of the American herds number more than a hundred animals, and there are now perhaps more Belties in America than in their native Galloway. New Zealand also has its Galloway Cattle Society which includes both Galloways and Belted Galloways. There are fifteen or sixteen breeders of Belties in the two islands. Belties have been established in Argentina since 1925, especially in the sub-tropical Entre Rios province, from which some have been exported to Brazil. In 1950 a strong herd was formed at Timau, Kenya, the bulls being used for crossing with the local Boran cattle, but I saw no Belties, though plenty of black Galloways, when visiting Timau in 1971.

From all countries where Belties are well established breeders return regularly to Scotland to replenish their herds with the best stock obtainable.

Description

The most distinctive feature of the Belted Galloway is the broad white band which encircles the middle part of the body. This characteristic is dominant, so that when a Belted bull is mated with a cow of any other breed, the belt is almost certain to appear in the progeny. In appearance and conformation the Beltie is very similar to the Galloway, with short legs, stocky body, broad head and no horns. In Scotland and other northern countries it grows a thick, wavy even shaggy coat of hair, but in warmer climates it dispenses with this. The colours, apart from the white belt, are black and, less commonly, dun. Do not coddle.

Uses

The Belted Galloway is primarily a beef breed, very hardy and adaptable. Even in extremely cold winters, such as those experienced in Quebec, it is not housed. Yet on the coarse pastures of sub-tropical northern Argentina, infested as they are with tick, the Belted Galloway has done exceptionally well. Cows when mature weigh around 500 to 600 kgs, bulls 750 to 950 kgs. When programme-fed the calves can put on weight quickly.

The cows are excellent mothers, with more milk than most beef cattle. Cows giving over 1000 gallons per lactation are not unknown, though perhaps 700 to 750 gallons is nearer the average. The milk is rich, with butterfat content of around 4%. Generally the cows are not milked but are allowed to rear their own calves, which they do very efficiently.

The Belted Galloway is a first-class crossing breed, in both sexes. Traditionally, the Beltie cows are mated with a Whitebred Shorthorn bull to produce the blue-grey belted calves so popular with fatteners. Recently they have been crossed with Simmental and Charolais bulls, with excellent results. The progeny of a Beltie parent is invariably polled. The female blue-greys usually inherit their milking qualities from their dam and make good mothers in their turn.

Belted Welsh Black

There are references in the eighteenth century to belted cattle in Wales, as there are to cattle of almost every other bovine colour or combination of colours. At Penrhyn Castle, Bangor, Lord Penrhyn had a herd of Belted Welsh Blacks which, around the time of their dispersal in 1907, numbered over 100 head and was said to have been in existence for over a century. Belted cattle, locally known as 'blanket' cattle, seem also to have been widely known in Caernarvonshire, Merionethshire and Denbighshire early in the present century. Local people had various explanations for the belted factor, including the importation, long before, of cows from Holland, or from France, or from Ireland; but it is at least as possible that the Belties are an indigenous type.

When in 1965 Lord David Stuart, gathering

material for his *An Illustrated History of Belted Cattle* (1970), toured North Wales he found fifteen farms within a fifteen-mile radius of Dolgellau where there were one or more Belted black cattle.

In 1975 the Rare Breeds Survival Trust reported that Belted Welsh Blacks were kept mainly on two farms in North Wales and that a Breed Society was being formed. In August, 1977, the formation of the Breed Society was still in the future, though a meeting to discuss the project was called in October of that year.

Description

Belted Welsh Black are apparently no more than colour-marked Welsh Blacks, which breed they seem to resemble in every other respect. On the other hand, it is worth recalling that Belted Galloways were originally considered to be merely colour-marked Galloways. The cattle are horned. The cows do not appear to have particularly thick coats and are generally housed in winter.

Uses

These differ in no way from those of the Welsh Blacks, which, however, are themselves a breed that has been vastly improved in recent years, especially as beef cattle. The belt is evidently a very persistent feature, for Lord David Stuart reports that Mr Dafydd Jones, of Beddcoedwr, Llanfachreth, had six or eight belted or partially belted animals in his herd of Welsh Blacks, although a belted bull had not been used for thirty years. For many years, because the Welsh Black Cattle Society refused to recognise the belted cattle and because the Belties had no breed society of their own, it was impossible to get a belted bull licensed for service, with the result that the numbers of belted cattle dwindled almost to vanishing point. But belted calves may be born to Welsh Black dams at any time.

A Welsh farmer told Lord David Stuart that the milk given by his Belted cattle was quite rich in butterfat and solids-not-fat.

Black-sided Tronder

This breed is more or less identical with the Swedish Mountain, though selection has been for a rather different colour pattern.

Present status

Becoming rare. The number of bulls has sunk very low.

Description

A small mountain breed, the males weighing up to 1700 pounds, the females 700 to 900 pounds. Whereas the Swedish cattle tend to be mostly white, with red markings, the Norwegian have their darker colour red rather than black, and many may be said to be black cattle with white markings. The white is usually along the spine, on the tail, and under the stomach. In specimens with white heads, the ears are black. The breed is normally polled.

Uses

Developed as a dairy breed. Well acclimatized to the harsh weather and rugged terrain of northern Norway, it can average up to 900 gallons of milk annually, with a high butterfat content.

Blanco-orejinegro

A breed found in mountain foot-hills in Colombia, South America. Ancestry unknown.

Present status

Declining.

Description

For some unexplained reason, this breed resembles in colour the British White and the Swedish Mountain breeds. Its Spanish name means the 'Black-eared White' breed, which accurately describes it. The basic colour is white but can be lightly or heavily mottled with black. Ears and muzzle are always black. Horns, medium, rather wide and upcurved. A rather light breed, mature bulls weighing up to 1300 pounds; cows averaging about 900 pounds.

Uses

Normally kept for beef.

Blue Albion

A Blue Albion Cattle Society was disbanded in 1975, though it had not been active since the beginning of the second world war. The Blue Albion originated from crosses between white Shorthorns and certain black cattle, most probably the Welsh Blacks, but only blue roan calves were considered typical of the breed and admitted to the Herd Books. However, the blue roans did not breed true but produced many throw-backs to their black or white ancestors, although if these blacks and whites were mated they were quite likely to produce blue roan progeny in their turn. So the Blue Albion was of doubtful validity as a breed.

Present status

At one time a number of herds existed, particularly in the Midlands and North, with 44 licensed bulls in the year 1935–36, but numbers dwindled until now there is probably only one surviving herd of any size. This is in Lancashire. It does, however, have two distinct sire lines, so material is available for a revival.

A favourite cross with fattening farms in northern England and southern Scotland is the Blue Grey, which is the result of a cross between a white Beef Shorthorn bull and a Galloway cow. This hybrid is not a Blue Albion, though it is similar in appearance.

Description

The Blue Albion is a dual-purpose animal, very similar to the Dairy Shorthorn but blue roan in colour.

Uses

The cows are said to give up to 6 gallons of milk a day and to maintain production well. Steers are useful beef animals and fatten quite quickly on an adequate ration.

23

Bretonne Pie-noire,

or BRITTANY BLACK-&-WHITE

An indigenous breed in southern Brittany.

Present status

Maintained as a pure breed in its native corner.

Description

Very like a small Friesian in colour and conformation. Bulls weight up to 1300 to 1500 pounds, cows 800 to 900 pounds. Horns small, curving upwards and forwards.

Uses

A very hardy dairy breed, used to poor pickings in the raw damp climate of a Breton winter. For its size it gives quite a lot of milk, up to 11,000 pounds per lactation at over 4% of butterfat.

British White

One suspects, though nothing is certain, that the British White is descended from an old type of white cattle which was either wild or feral in Britain fifteen hundred years ago.

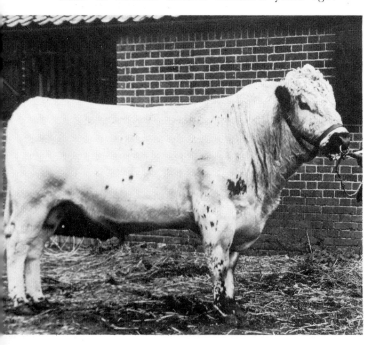

Some relationship exists between it and the herds of wild white cattle which survive at Chillingham (for which see *White Park*) and elsewhere, although the wild white cattle are horned, whereas the British White is polled.

The breed, which seems to have once been widely distributed, though strongest in East Anglia, was becoming rare when its breed society was formed soon after the first world war. In the second world war, in order to safeguard the future of the breed, a group of representative cattle were sent to Bronx Zoo in New York. From there they were taken to the King Ranch in Texas, which had more space and better facilities for dealing with them, and there a small herd still flourishes. At one time a few British Whites were exported to Colombia, and others have followed them more recently. There have also been some exports to Kenya.

Controversy exists as to whether the white cattle of early times were really indigenous or were imported from Italy by the Romans. There are traditions that before the Romans came the Celtic Druids sacrificed white

cattle to certain gods. On the other hand, the British White is very similar to the Swedish Mountain breed, which is still found, though in decreasing numbers, in the northern provinces of Sweden, and, in view of the former concentration of the breed in East Anglia, the possibility that it was introduced by Vikings in the Dark Ages must obviously be considered.

In the late 1940s I was familiar with the breed on the Norfolk farm of the late Colonel Quentin Gurney. Now the breed's largest herd is still located in Norfolk, at Rippon Hall, near Norwich, where Miss Caroline and Miss Diana Birkbeck own the fine Hevingham herd, with over 50 breeding cows.

Present status

Membership of the British White breed society has nearly doubled in the past few years, standing at 29 recently. Three distinct bloodlines within the breed are being maintained, and semen is available from some of the best bulls. Classes for British Whites at the Royal Norfolk Show, which was the breed's main shop-window, were discontinued in around 1965, but the breed has appeared at the Trust's shows and sales, and open days have been held at Rippon Hall.

Description

The British White is a dual-purpose breed. In conformation it closely resembles the Dairy Shorthorn. The colour is white, with black ears, noses, eyelashes and feet and with sometimes black flecks on other parts of the hide. The breed is always polled. British Whites are completely hardy.

Uses

The British White can be fairly described as an undeveloped dual-purpose breed. Its performance is on a par with that of a good average Dairy Shorthorn. The British Whites in Colonel Gurney's herd used to produce about 800 gallons of milk, with a butterfat content of 4%, per lactation without difficulty. For beef production the Hevingham British Whites attain weights of 8 to 9 cwt on an economical diet. Their crossing potential has yet to be thoroughly explored but the evidence of first-crosses indicates that it is very considerable, and British White bulls 'mark' their progeny. The breed is very docile.

Camargue

The fighting cattle of the Camargue country, in the delta of the Rhone.

Present status

A semi-wild breed, maintained for the sport it gives at festival time in the arenas of southern France, such as that at Arles. Probably numbers around 25,000.

Description

A lithe, slender, agile breed, with heavy shoulders and light hindquarters. Colour, black. Horns, long and up-curved. Has an alert, aggressive manner. Bulls weigh up to 800 to 900 pounds; cows, 650 to 750 pounds.

Uses

Entirely for sport. Before the bull enters the arena a garland or ribbon is tied between his horns, and the sport is for men on foot to try to snatch it from him. There is no fight as such, and the bull is not killed — indeed, the same bull is brought in to perform time and again. Only the bulls are used. The cows are never milked, and only animals too old for the arena or for breeding are slaughtered.

Criollo

This is not so much a breed as a type of cattle evolved by natural selection. Criollos are found in every Spanish-American and Portuguese-American country and are descended from Spanish or Portuguese cattle introduced centuries ago. Over the years they have become thoroughly acclimatised and capable of resisting the diseases, parasites and stresses of tropical and sub-tropical climates. They have thus presented excellent foundation stock on which to base improvements.

Some have been developed in one direction, some in another. A milking strain is found chiefly in Colombia and neighbouring republics. The Cuban Criollo has developed as a useful dual-purpose breed. In much of South America Criollos have been replaced by European breeds, by zebu breeds from India, and by the excellent American Santa Gertrudis breed.

While the Criollo can hardly as yet be termed a rare breed, it does tend to disappear quite rapidly when confronted with competition from more highly specialised breeds. In some countries it is now confined to remote and little developed regions. Genetically it has so much to offer that schemes should be evolved soon to ensure that it never becomes extinct.

De Lidia

This is the breed that provides bulls for the arena, both in Spain and in Spanish-American countries.

Present status Unthreatened.

Description

Colour, black or deep grey. Horns, wide and curving outward, forward and upward. The forequarters are much heavier than the hindquarters. Bulls weigh up to 1600 pounds, but most of those which appear in the ring are around 1200 pounds; cows weigh about 1000 pounds.

Uses

Selection is solely for the purpose of producing aggressive, alert and fast-moving bulls for the arenas.

Dexter

While the origins of the Dexter breed are obscure, the breed is thought to have been deliberately developed by selection. Small farmers of southern Ireland apparently preferred small animals and therefore chose to breed from the smallest of their aboriginal, Kerry-type cattle. At some time it is suggested that the miniature size was more firmly established by the introduction of animals with a dwarf gene, probably from North Africa or Portugal.

Dexters are known to have existed in Ireland in the late eighteenth century. The first recorded exports to England were made in 1882, and the English Dexter Herd Book was started in 1900. The tiny, compact, sprightly Dexter became a popular house cow on country estates in England but its popularity declined in Ireland, where the Herd Book ceased publication in 1919.

The Dexter has become associated with the phenomenon known as 'bulldog' calves. A proportion of calves is born with a squashed 'bulldog' face, and these have to be destroyed. The deformity is associated with the dwarfing gene. The incidence of 'bulldog' calf births is subject to some controversy, varying as it does according to the strain and type of Dexter involved. It is sometimes put as high as 25%, but this is disputed by some breeders, especially by those who are trying to breed out the weakness.

Present status

In 1975–6 261 births were recorded in the English Dexter Herd Book, of which 17 were to non-Dexter bulls. The total strength of the breed in England is almost certainly less than 400. It will be gathered from the above that not all the entries in the Herd Book are of pure animals.

The breed is fairly well represented in U.S.A. and probably in South Africa. In Ireland it apparently declined to vanishing point, but small numbers have been re-introduced recently, primarily for experimental work. Incidentally, this group has produced only 8% of 'bulldog' calves, which is much lower than the generally quoted figure.

Description

The colour is normally black, but occasionally dark-red animals occur, and some breeders are re-introducing dun, which seems to have been one of the original colours. The Dexter is the smallest breed found in the British Isles, the

Flamande bull

Flamande

A large breed once widely distributed on the French side of the French-Belgium border.

Present status

Declining rapidly, in competition with the Friesian.

Description

A large, heavy breed, dark brown or black in colour. Bulls weigh up to 2500 pounds; cows 1300 to 1500 pounds. Horns thin and forward curving in cows; short and almost straight in the bulls.

Uses

Dual-purpose. Has considerable potential for both milk and beef production which, however, has not been fully developed, and so the breed has fallen behind the other main French breeds.

cows weighing from 600 to 650 pounds, the bulls up to 900 or 1000 pounds. The body is deep and the legs short. Some breeders suggest that the 'bulldog' deformity is connected with attempts to breed for even smaller and shorter-legged types, resulting in dwarf rather than miniature cattle. Most Dexters stand no higher than 44 inches at the withers, though some of the longer-legged types reach 47 inches. The Dexter excels as a house-cow or smallholder's animal, being a useful scavenger and thriving on a miscellaneous diet. It is hardy and can be out-wintered in many districts.

Uses

The Dexter is a dual-purpose breed. Its chief claim to distinction is its efficiency in converting food into either milk or meat. According to some authorities, it needs only about 60% of the food required by a Friesian; according to others its requirements are nearer 40%. Its average milk yield is about 500 gallons per lactation, 4% butterfat, but the best can do considerably better, some over 1000 gallons. Longevity is a characteristic of the Dexter, and the cows take readily to the multiple suckling of calves. The small joints of the Dexter carcase make them ideal for a family deep-freeze.

Florida Scrub

These were small nondescript cattle that moved into Florida with the Spaniards from the sixteenth century onwards. Many ran wild and many were rounded up and kept by Indian tribes. When the United States purchased Florida in 1819 the country was well populated with this type of cattle.

Present status

Nearing extinction, but a few probably survive.

Description

Small, light, long-legged cattle, with rather slender horns of medium size. Colour, very variable. Weights attained by cows were often not more than 500 or 600 pounds.

Uses

The Florida Scrub possesses, or possessed, only one major asset. Through many generations of natural selection it had developed a resistance to screw-worm, fever tick and all the other parasites and ailments endemic in that sub-tropical climate. It constitutes a valuable heredity, and one worth preserving.

Fribourg Black and White

Once widely distributed in Switzerland but now probably confined to the canton of Fribourg.

Present status

Disappearing. Owing to extensive crossing with Friesians, numbers of pure bred cows are very low, and no bulls remain.

Description

A black-and-white cow with conformation very like that of the Simmenthal, from which it probably derived and was separated by selection for colour. It is not therefore closely related to the Friesian, which it resembles in colour. Mature bulls weigh up to 2500 pounds; cows 1300 to 1700 pounds.

Uses

Dual-purpose, with an emphasis on milk production.

Fribourg Black and White

Grey Alpine, ————

GREY MOUNTAIN or GRAUVIEH

A primitive and perhaps indigenous breed in the mountains of Central Europe, especially in the Tyrol and adjacent valleys in Austria and Italy.

Present status

Not common even in its native provinces, but probably safe from extinction because it is so well adapted to life in those austere mountain regions.

Description

Grey with light and dark shading on different parts of the body. The bulls bear a certain resemblance to Jerseys. Horns, long and more up-curved in cows than in bulls.

Uses

Dual-purpose, but primarily a dairy animal, with a high butterfat content to its milk.

Grey Steppe

A formerly widespread indigenous breed in S.E. Europe.

Present status

Gradually disappearing as more productive breeds are introduced. Several other breeds in S.E. Europe, such as the *Iskur* of Bulgaria and the native Greek cattle, are derived from crosses between the Grey Steppe cattle and other breeds. In Turkey they with their crosses may still account for about 10% of the cattle population.

Description

Medium sized. The females are light grey, with fairly long, up-turned horns, and weigh 700 to 900 pounds. The bulls are a much darker grey, shading to black on the shoulders, with long crescent-shaped horns, and weigh up to 1400 pounds.

Uses

Originally bred primarily for draught purposes. Now being developed for milk and meat. Milk yields are low but butterfat contents high.

Groningen

The breed originated in the province of Groningen, in the north-eastern Netherlands but is now found in other parts of the country as well.

Present status

In 1968 numbered approximately 75,000, but, of course, far outnumbered in the Netherlands by black-and-white Friesians.

Description

Usually black, with a white head and some white on the underparts but with a black ring around the eyes. In a minority of animals the black is replaced by red. Horns short, with a tendency to curve downwards. Bulls weigh around 2200 to 2500 pounds; cows, 1500 to 1600 pounds.

Uses

Dual-purpose. It approaches the Friesian in both milk and beef production without actually overtaking it.

Hawaiian Wild

These cattle are descended from Mexican Criollos introduced at the end of the eighteenth century. Some of these had been kept in ranches but others had escaped to the bush and gone wild. When improved European breeds were introduced there was some interbreeding, but the old Spanish-American type still predominated.

In 1925 a campaign to round up and eradicate the wild cattle began and continued until only one herd was left.

Present status

A wild herd roams over about 40,000 acres of the McCandless Ranch in the south-western part of Hawaii. A recent estimate is that there are about 2000 of them.

Description

Light, nondescript, long-legged animals. Colours, very variable. Horns, long, spreading and upturned. Bulls weigh up to 1200 pounds, cows 600 to 800 pounds. The breed is light on the hindquarters and is agile and nervous.

Uses

By natural selection is highly resistant to parasites and diseases. Little practical use is at present made of the breed, but some of the young animals occasionally appear in rodeos.

Herens, or ERINGER

An indigenous breed of the Herens valley, in Switzerland.

Present status

Low in numbers but in no immediate danger of extinction. A herd book is being well maintained.

Description

A very small breed, rather larger than but something like the Dexter. The bulls weigh up to 1300 pounds, the cows 900 to 1000 pounds. Colour, dull black, with traces of red on hips and along spine. Horns, medium, longer in cows than in bulls and well up-curved.

Uses

Ostensibly this is a dairy breed. The milk yield is around 6500 to 7500 pounds per lactation, with a fairly high butterfat content. The breed probably owes its continued existence, however, to the fact that it traditionally produces fighting cows, who do battle with each other on festival days. Cow fights are regarded as notable occasions, and the cows are specially groomed and trained for them. Oddly, only the cows are matched against each other, never the bulls.

Irish Dun

Cattle reputed to be descended from imports by the Vikings, but now stated to be indistinguishable from the Shorthorn, except for colour.

Present status

In a survey in 1974 the Rare Breeds Survival Trust reported the existence of three cows of the right colour, but no bulls. In December, 1975, it regretfully concluded that the breed must be considered extinct.

Description

A breed very similar to, if not identical with, the Shorthorn, but polled. Colour, dun.

Uses

Stated by Low in 1842 as being a potentially excellent dairy breed.

33

Irish Moyled

Irish Moyled

The Irish Moyled is an ancient breed, reputed to be descended from cattle brought to Ireland by the Vikings.

Present status

One large herd survives, apart from which odd cattle are to be found in herds of other breeds, chiefly in Ulster. A bull of the Finnish Poll breed, imported to Belfast in, it is believed, about 1947, was said to have been intended for crossing with Irish Moyled cows.

Description

The basic colour is a purplish roan, very similar to that of the Longhorn, but with a broad white dorsal stripe, a white tail and much white on the underparts, legs and face. The breed is polled, 'moyle' or 'mael' meaning 'hornless'.

Uses

Dual-purpose, originally draught and milk.

Kerry

The Kerry takes its name from the south-westernmost county of Ireland but was evidently once widely distributed in that country, and it may well be descended from indigenous stock in prehistoric times. The skeletons of cattle found in Early Bronze Age burial tumuli in Britain are very similar to that of a small Kerry. In Ireland they were kept purest in the south-west, the region farthest from English influence, where they were regarded as the poor man's cattle. Towards the end of the eighteenth century the Irish cattle which were then coming over to England in considerable numbers were called Kerries but were larger than the aboriginal stock through the influence of imported bulls of Bakewell's Longhorns. In the nineteenth century there was much crossing with imported Shorthorns. But in the middle of the present century efforts were being made to keep the breed pure and reasonably strong, only Kerry bulls being licensed for use in the south-west.

In Britain the Kerry was in favour chiefly as a park cow and as a house cow on country estates.

Present status

In Britain the Kerry is in eclipse, the British

Kerry Society having been dissolved in the late 1960s. In Ireland a breed society still exists, has some enthusiastic breeders and is regarded with favour by the Irish Government, which owns one of the largest surviving herds. However, an estimate of the strength of the breed in Ireland in 1976 put the total number of cows at no more than 234.

Description

The Kerry is a small, black breed, the cows lightly built and of dairy type. Occasionally there is a little white on the udder. A hundred years ago their coloration was more variable and included brown, black and mixtures of the two, with often a white streak on the belly and sometimes a white "finching" stripe, like the Longhorn. The breed is horned, the horns being white with black tips.

The instances given above show that if beef is wanted the Kerry responds well to generous treatment. When kept primarily for milk, however, which is usual, it does well on poor or moderate grazing. It is an economical converter of food, at whatever level. And it is hardy.

Uses

Dual-purpose, for the breed was used for every purpose in its homeland. However, it is primarily a dairy animal. A good cow will yield perhaps 800 gallons per lactation but will continue to do so for many years, for longevity is one of its characteristics. The butterfat content is generally about 4%. The milk has small globules, which make it easily digestible. Under really good conditions the Kerry can achieve quite high yields — 1500 gallons or more — but it has been traditionally kept on poor pastures in mountains and boggy land.

Under favourable conditions, too, the breed is no mean performer as a beef animal. After the first world war some Kerries sent to help in the rehabilitation of the devastated regions of north-eastern France were set to graze in rich pastures by the river Somme. Within nine months they had put on weight to such an extent that the French, disappointed that their milk yields had not increased to match, sold them off as beef cattle and reported very favourably on their beefing qualities. Recent experiments with crossing Kerry cows with Charolais bulls have proved very satisfactory, the progeny putting on weight quickly. The incidence of difficult calvings, in spite of the disparity in size of the two breeds, is very low.

Lakenvelder,———

or DUTCH BELTED

The Lakenvelder seem to have originated in the Netherlands, where, at any rate, they were plentiful in the eighteenth and nineteenth centuries. When the improved Friesians became dominant, many landowners preserved Lakenvelder as picturesque features of their country parks. When eventually a Herd Book was formed in 1918 it was estimated that about 300 cattle remained in the country, in the hands of twelve to fifteen breeders. In spite of this, the numbers continued to decline, and the Herd Book was closed in 1931. The Lakenvelder had to contend with two impediments not unknown in other countries. In the first place, when bull licensing was in force (from 1950 to 1959) it was forbidden to keep a bull which was not registered with the Dutch Herd Book Society, and the Lakenvelder had no breed Herd Book to represent them. Fortunately, one breeder at least was granted a special licence. Later, considerable numbers of Lakenvelder failed to pass the tuberculosis test and had to be slaughtered. When Lord David Stuart visited Holland in 1961 to collect material for his book *An Illustrated History of Belted Cattle* he found only three breeders left. The largest herd had two belted bulls and twelve females.

However, the Lakenvelder had meantime taken root in a new country, the United States of America, where by the end of the nineteenth century they were well established. There are records of imports as early as 1838, though others may well have occurred earlier, and in 1848 a Mr H. W. Coleman, of Cornwall, Pennsylvania, is reported to have brought in a large herd of Lakenvelder from Holland.

Present status

There are still Lakenvelder in the Netherlands, though the numbers are few. They should now be safe from extinction, for, after much preliminary work, an organisation similar to the Rare Breeds Survival Trust was formed in February, 1976. It is thought, however, that the Dutch Lakenvelder may have been modified over the years, through having been kept primarily as park or 'hobby' cattle, and that the American Dutch Belted cattle may be nearer the original type.

In the U.S.A. the Dutch Belted hardly qualifies for inclusion in this book, for it is by no means a rare breed. It is well distributed in the States and has spread over the borders into Canada and Mexico. In 1970 the Dutch Belted Cattle Association of America had twenty members, but some of the herds were large, that of the President of the Association, Mr J.G. DuPuis, Jr, of Roselawn Farm, Miami, Florida, including over 300 Dutch Belted milking cows.

Description

The distinctive white belt of the Lakenvelder can be on either a black or a red ground. In conformation the breed resembles the Dairy Shorthorn and, in many respects, the Guernsey, though it is rather larger and heavier than the latter. The Lakenvelder is a horned breed, the horns being normally curved upwards at the points. In America the Dutch Belted have tended to gravitate to the southern states, where they undoubtedly do well on fertile pastures, and hence they seem to have acquired a reputation for being not quite as hardy as some other breeds. However, herds in the northern states and in Canada seem to be well adapted to life there.

Uses

The Dutch Belted, and the Lakenvelder from which it sprang, is a dairy breed. The American Association gives the average weight of mature bulls as 1400 to 2000 pounds, and of mature cows as 900 to 1500 pounds. The milk is moderately rich in butterfat. Dutch breeders with Lakenvelder and Friesians in the same herd say that the milk yields of the two breeds are about the same.

Longhorn

Until the eighteenth century unimproved Longhorns were abundant and widespread throughout Midland and northern England. They were the breed selected by the great pioneers of livestock breeding, notably Webster of Canley and Robert Bakewell, for their early experiments.

The Longhorn was originally regarded as an all-purpose breed. It was a heavy, powerful, docile animal, suitable for work on the land. It produced a satisfactory carcase on a large farm. Its milk yields were not remarkably high, but the milk had a high cream and solids content and was particularly suitable for the making of cheese.

Bakewell and his disciples concentrated on improving the meat-producing potential of the Longhorn, sacrificing some of its other qualities in the process. Also, although the breed was specially suited to fattening on the rich pastures of the Midlands, it took a long time about it. In consequence, it gradually lost ground to faster-maturing beef breeds, such as the Beef Shorthorn and Aberdeen-Angus, and to dual-purpose breeds, such as the Dairy Shorthorn.

Present status

In the 1960s the breed was reduced to only a few herds and only a few hundred cattle. Since then the situation has been stabilised,

and the Longhorns are in no danger of extinction, though their numbers are still low.

Description

A massive, powerful animal. Body, long but moderately deep. Legs, rather short. Horns, long and usually down-curved, giving the animal a somewhat menacing appearance, completely contradicted by its docile nature. Colour, brindle, often with a bluish tinge; tail and stripe along back, white; also some white on legs and dewlap and often a white patch on flank.

No special treatment needed. The breed is very hardy.

Uses

Primarily a superb beef breed. It will still fatten on good grass, but if programme-fed indoors it will put on weight at rates comparable with any other breed. The quality of the beef is excellent. Longhorn cattle consistently win prizes at Birmingham Christmas Fatstock Shows.

Milk yields are not heavy, but the milk is very rich, with more than twice the butterfat content of many other breeds.

37

Mantequera Leonesa

An indigenous breed of the province of Leon, in north-western Spain.

Present status Probably in no danger.

Description

A reddish-brown breed with dairying conformation. Horns, short but growing forward and outward. Rather leggy.

Uses

Traditionally a draught animal but has been developed to some extent as a milk producer.

Mertolenga

A breed of southern Portugal, taking its name from the town of Mertola, near the Spanish border.

Present status

Probably satisfactory, for it is being improved as a beef breed.

Description

Dark brown in colour with occasional white markings. Horns, spreading, long and up-curved. Bulls weigh 1600 to 1800 pounds; cows, 1000 to 1200 pounds.

Uses

Formerly a draught animal but now being developed for beef.

Modenese

A breed of ancient origins in the Po valley, in northern Italy.

Present status

Probably satisfactory.

Description

Very similar to the Romagnola, which originates in the same part of Italy, but the colour is white instead of grey.

Uses

Has been developed largely as a milk producer but has good beef potential.

Modicana

Early in the Middle Ages an epidemic is said to have wiped out the native cattle of Sicily. Imports were made to fill the gap. Their source is uncertain, but the likeliest explanation is that they came from northern Europe, Sicily being then governed by Norman kings. The theory is fortified by the fact that the Modicana show similarities to the Danish Red and crosses with it readily. They are unlike any of the breeds of mainland Italy.

Present status

Probably satisfactory.

Description

Dark red in colour. Fairly heavily built. Horns long and up-curved in cow; shorter and almost straight in bull. Bulls weigh up to 1600 pounds; cows from 900 to 1300 pounds, much depending on their rations.

Uses

All-purpose, with an emphasis on draught and milk. Their real potential has, however, not yet been developed.

Murciana

The indigenous breed of Murcia province, in south-eastern Spain.

Present status

Still widespread in its homeland.

Description

A rather large, heavy breed, with heavier forequarters than hindquarters. Colour, deep chestnut, though lighter on some parts of the body. The face is sometimes black-spotted.

39

MURCIANA

Horns, short and down-curved. Bulls weigh up to 1800 pounds; cows to 1200 pounds.

Uses

Traditionally a draught animal. Largely undeveloped for modern markets.

North Finncattle

More or less identical with the Swedish Mountain and Black-sided Tronder.

Present status

It is doubtful whether any cattle of this type remain in Finland.

Murnau-Werdenfelser

A breed originating in Austria but latterly concentrated around the towns of Murnau and Werdenfels, at the foot of the Bavarian Alps.

Present status

Unknown but probably low in numbers. Only 22,000 remained in 1967.

Description

A soft mushroom-brown in colour, as with the Brown Swiss, which it resembles. Bulls weigh around 1800 pounds; cows from 1100 to 1300 pounds.

Uses

Originally an all-purpose breed, kept largely for draught purposes but latterly for beef and milk. Although useful milkers, their yields are not as high as those of the Brown Swiss.

40

Northern Dairy Shorthorn

The Northern Dairy Shorthorn comes from the same stock as was used in the late eighteenth century by the Collings Brothers in the development of the Teeswater breed, afterwards the Shorthorn. As is well known, the breed later split into the Dairy and Beef Shorthorns. Meantime, the Northern Dairy Shorthorn evolved on similar lines to the Dairy Shorthorn in the dales of the Pennines. Although not recognised as a separate breed and with no breed society until 1944, the Northern Dairy Shorthorn was kept pure through many generations by the interchange of bulls between farmers in the dales.

Present status

The Northern Dairy Shorthorn is, of course, a Dairy Shorthorn, and so it was logical that in due course its records should be incorporated in Coates Herd Book, the official organ of the Dairy Shorthorn Society. This happened in 1969, with the inevitable risk that the breed would lose its identity and become fully merged with the Dairy Shorthorn. Some breeders, however, consider that it is worth maintaining as a distinct breed. A recent estimate is that about 250 cows but no more than six bulls of the breed remain. There are at present 14 breeders.

Description

Similar to the Dairy Shorthorn but almost always roan, with the body and hindquarters much lighter in colour than the head and forequarters. It is longer in the leg than some Shorthorns and holds itself alert, with head erect. There may possibly be a touch of Ayrshire in its ancestry.

Bred in the cold northern dales, the Northern Dairy Shorthorn is very hardy. It can outwinter and produce milk on rough grazing and home-produced rations. Some breeders maintain that it is the best breed available for local conditions.

Uses

The Northern Dairy Shorthorn was developed as a dairy breed, and particularly for supplying milk for the making of farmhouse butter and cheese on upland farms. While it cannot compete with the yields of modern specialist dairy breeds it can maintain herd averages of over 1000 gallons, and there have been individual records of more than 2000 gallons. Beef is a useful secondary product.

Old Gloucestershire

At one time the Old Gloucestershire breed or type was dominant on either side of the lower estuary of the river Severn, not only in the county of Gloucestershire but in north Somerset, Monmouthshire and neighbouring shires, while the now extinct Glamorgan cattle, very similar in appearance, were almost certainly derived from the Gloucestershires. Even towards the end of the eighteenth century, however, they were becoming scarce, for J. Lawrence, writing in 1809, comments that they were "difficult to find". Its long decline seems to have begun with the beginning of the Age of Improvement and was, in the first place, probably due to competition from the improved Longhorn, and later the Shorthorn. Like all cattle in early days, the Gloucestershire had to take its place as an all-purpose breed, and as late as the 1770s a team of Gloucestershire oxen was transported to his estates in Essex by a Lord Clare.

Farther back in time, cattle of the Gloucestershire type were evidently long established in their homeland and may well be indigenous, and the description that Lord David Stuart, in his *An Illustrated History of Belted Cattle* (1970), gives of the aboriginal cattle of Ayrshire, Clydesdale, Peebleshire and the islands of Arran and Bute, namely that they were "black, striped with white along their backs and about their flanks and faces, while their horns were high and crooked", shows that they must have been akin to the Gloucestershire.

By 1958 there were only three herds of the breed left. In 1966 the largest of all the herds, one of 148 cattle belonging to Mr Ralph Bathurst, was put up for auction on his death. The upheaval may well have proved the salvation of the breed, for at least five new breeders acquired enough stock to run a pure herd and expressed their intention of doing so. Included in the sale was a fine bull, Brewer, stated at the time to be "thought to be the only remaining pure-bred bull in this country"; though there is a doubt as to whether even he was pure, for experiments in crossing the Bathurst Gloucestershire with Shorthorns had been made some thirty or forty years earlier.

Through all these vicissitudes the breed was maintained by one stalwart, the late Mr R. Dowdeswell, of Wick Court, Saul, Gloucestershire, whom I knew well and often visited. In the early 1960s I noted that he had 14 Gloucestershire cows in milk and one bull, with followers to make up a total herd of 40 to 50 head. After his death this herd was dispersed in 1972, but again new owners desiring to start herds came forward, and in 1973 the Gloucestershire Cattle Society, which had lapsed in 1945, was re-formed.

Present status

The breed is now safe from extinction, barring unforeseen disasters. In 1974 the Society had 38 members, with 20 herds, comprising about 70 animals in the full register, and the numbers have subsequently increased. Semen from Gloucestershire bulls is available for A.I.

Description

The most conspicuous feature of the Gloucestershire breed is the "finching" or white dorsal stripe which extends to the white tail. There is sometimes white on the flanks and always on the belly and underparts. The ground colour is officially described as deep mahogany brown; some of the bulls are almost black. The breed is horned.

My first sight of the Old Gloucestershires on the estate of the late Colonel Elwes, at Colesbourne, Gloucestershire, many years ago, provided a remarkable insight into the protective value of the breed's coloration and especially of the white finching stripe. I was looking at a group of young heifers, lighter in colour than the mature cows, when suddenly they took fright and cantered away into a covert of dead bracken. Their ground colour blended so well with the fern as to make them almost invisible, but the white stripe and tail flashed out a conspicuous warning, just like the white scut of a rabbit and the white tails of several species of deer. The coloration is undoubtedly of very ancient origin, probably developed in the wild.

Uses

The Old Gloucestershire breed was, although dual-purpose or all-purpose, especially noted for the quality of its milk, which, because of the small size of its fat globules, was particularly suited for the making of the famous Double Gloucester cheese. It is perhaps because its breeders chose the wrong speciality that the breed declined. The milk yields were not high. Mr Dowdeswell used to estimate that the average for his cows was between 700 and 800 per lactation, but the Bathurst herd had an average of 926 gallons at 3.74% butterfat.

Interest is now veering towards the beef potentialities of the breed. In a recent test a pure-bred bull achieved a daily gain in weight of 3.5 pounds, weighing out at 1202 pounds at 400 days, which puts it on a level with many beef breeds. Some breeders, however, are maintaining the milk production of their herds and comment that the Gloucestershire seems to have no peak to its lactation but continues to produce a level flow of milk for month after month.

The breed is hardy and adapts well to rather rough, coarse grazing. Although traditionally kept in the rich pastures of the Severn valley it could be well suited to upland farming.

Piedmontese

A native breed of the Po valley in Piedmont, in north-west Italy.

Present status

Believed satisfactory, but numbers are decreasing.

Description

Very similar to the Romagnola but smaller. The colour is creamy-grey. Bulls weigh up to 2000 pounds; cows 1200 to 1500 pounds.

Uses

Originally all-purpose but primarily a draught animal. Now kept chiefly for beef.

Pinzgauer

This breed was developed in the Pinzgau Valley of Austria, from where it spread till it was widely distributed in the old Austro-Hungarian Empire. Its original role was as a working animal. Later it was reckoned to be a milk animal but, as with so many other breeds, interest has recently been diverted to its beef potential.

Pinzgauer

Present status

The breed is said to account for some 13% of the total cattle population of Austria. It is also found in southern Germany, Czechoslovakia and Yugoslavia. In 1976 a small group was introduced to Britain, from apparently mixed motives. Some breeders had the idea of reinforcing the Old Gloucestershire breed by crossing with the very similar Pinzgauer, but the Rare Breeds Survival Trust warned against this because the two breeds, although they have the same colour markings, are not related.

Description

The body colour is deep brown or red, with a white dorsal stripe ('finching') as in the Old Gloucestershire breed. However, this stripe is

44

Pirenaica

much wider than in the Old Gloucestershire, becoming wider towards the rump and extending in a patch of jagged outline over the rear end and hips. The tail is white, and there is also a white underline which often extends across the upper parts of the legs and some distance up the sides. The breed is horned.

The breed is very hardy, as might be expected of cattle traditionally bred for land-work in the rather severe climate of central Europe.

Uses

The Pinzgauer tends to be somewhat heavier than the Old Gloucestershire, bulls reaching weights of 2400 pounds and mature cows 1300 to 1550 pounds. Milk yields are moderate, around 700 to 800 gallons, but the milk is rich in butterfat (usually around 4%). The young animals respond well to programme-feeding and put on flesh efficiently.

Pirenaica

The indigenous breed of the Pyrenean mountain country of northern Spain.

Present status

Probably satisfactory.

Description

A large, dairy-type animal. Colour, from golden-red to creamy-white, the variation being governed largely by altitude. Horns, small and curved forward. Bulls weigh up to 2000 pounds; cows 1200 to 1600 pounds.

Uses

Traditionally a draught animal, but the milking potential of the breed, now being well developed, proves to be good.

45

Polish Red

Traditional indigenous breed of much of Poland.

Present status

Probably pure animals are now rare, the breed having extensively interbred with the Danish Red. A cross incorporating five-eighths Danish Red and three-eighths Polish Red has now been fixed and is considered to be a distinct breed.

Description

An all-red breed of dairy type. Bulls weigh up to 1800 pounds; cows, 1000 to 1100 pounds. Horns, short; curved forward in the female, nearly straight in the male.

Uses

Primarily a milk-producing breed, but as yields are rather low (7500 to 9000 pounds per lactation) crossing with Danish Reds has been introduced as a means of improving it.

Prete

Descended from animals introduced into Sicily in Norman times, after an epidemic had virtually wiped out the native cattle. Their origin is unknown.

Present status

Quite plentiful on the peasant farms of Sicily.

Description

A small, black breed. Horns long and up-curved in cow; shorter but still up-curved in bull. Bulls weigh up to 1000 pounds; cows, 700 to 800 pounds.

Uses

All-purpose, especially draught. Milk production is low but the breed has never been developed.

Red Polled Estland

This is a breed based on the indigenous cattle of south-eastern Norway, improved at various times by the introduction of Ayrshire, Friesian and Angler bulls.

Present status

Now probably submerged by the Norwegian Red Cattle.

Description

Colour, brownish red with sometimes a few white markings. Polled. Bulls weigh 1500 to 1700 pounds; cows, 1000 to 1200 pounds.

Uses

Dual-purpose.

Reggiana

Reggiana

Has its origins in the indigenous cattle of the Po valley around Reggio.

Present status

Probably satisfactory.

Description

Colour, a dark yellowish brown, with some white on underparts and on legs. Horns, short. Stands rather high on the legs. Bulls weigh 1700 to 1900 pounds; cows 1200 to 1400 pounds.

Uses

Although developed as an all-purpose breed with an emphasis on its draught potential, the Reggiana has long been associated with Parmesan cheese, which is made in this region of Italy. Local opinion insists that the best cheese can be made only from milk of this breed. The Reggiana is probably the best of the native Italian breeds for milk production. It also produces satisfactory bull beef.

48

Retinta Andaluza

The indigenous cattle of Andalucia, in southern Spain.

Present status

Probably in no danger.

Description

A big, heavy breed, with forequarters tending to be heavier than the hindquarters. Horns spread wide and are up-curved at the ends. Colour, dark red, but there is also a black variety, the *Negra Andaluza*.

Uses

Traditionally a draught animal but its beef potential is now being developed.

The breed is illustrated above right.

Rhodopska

An indigenous mountain breed in southern Bulgaria.

Present status

Confined to its native valleys and probably decreasing in numbers. There has been a little experimental crossing with the Jersey.

Description

A small, hardy animal, grey to blackish in colour, with the shoulders normally darker than the rest of the body. Horned. Males weigh up to 800 pounds; females to 500 pounds.

Uses

All-purpose, especially draught. Is considered to have good milking potential but has been little developed. Butterfat content of milk, high.

49

Romagnola

A large breed developed primarily for draught purposes in the Po valley of Italy.

Present status

Still quite plentiful in Italy, and has been exported to a number of other European countries, including Britain.

Description

Bulls weigh up to 2500 to 3000 pounds; cows around 1500 to 1700 pounds. Well muscled to match. Colour, light grey, with darker grey on shoulders of male, with black patches around eyes, and with black tailbrush. Horns, fairly long and up-curved.

Uses

Now that it is needed not nearly as extensively for draught purposes it has been developed as a beef breed. Exported animals are for crossing with dairy breeds, to produce beef from surplus animals from milking herds.

Romo-sinuana

A breed of northern Colombia, in South America. Ancestry unknown.

Present status

Unknown.

Description

Although related to the Criollo cattle of South America, this breed has the unusual characteristic (for Spanish and Spanish American breeds) of being polled. Brownish red in colour. Has good beef conformation but is rather small. Bulls weigh up to 1100 pounds; cows 700 to 900 pounds.

Uses

Primarily for beef.

Rotvieh

An indigenous breed of the mountains of central Germany.

Present status

Has greatly declined in numbers through competition with more productive breeds.

Description

Deep red or dark brown colour. Bulls weigh around 2100 pounds; cows from 1100 to 1400 pounds.

Uses

A draught breed converted to dual-purpose. As a milk producer it is a moderate performer, yielding some 8000 to 8500 pounds of milk at 4.1% butterfat per lactation, but it is in competition with others that can do better.

Rubia Gallega

An indigenous breed in north-western Spain.

Present status

Probably rather shaky, as it becomes superseded by more productive imported breeds.

Description

Light brownish-red in colour. Horns, long and curved outwards and upwards.

Uses

As with most Spanish breeds, was originally all-purpose, with an emphasis on draught. There has been some development of its milking potential, which appears to be good.

Salers

A mountain breed from the Auvergne, in south central France. Used to hard living on sparse mountain pastures.

Present status

Believed satisfactory. The breed has been taken in hand and improved.

Description

A rather heavy, dark red breed. The bulls weigh up to 2800 pounds; the cows, 1300 to 1700 pounds. Horns, rather large and curved upwards and forwards. The conformation is that of a beef breed.

Uses

Developed as a dual-purpose breed. Milk yields moderate with fairly high butterfat content.

Shetland

It is possible that the austere climate and meagre diet gradually produced a diminution in size of the Shetland cattle in their wind-swept northern islands. They are now the smallest British breed but one, the exception being the Dexter. The Shetland is thought to be of Scandinavian origin. A Herd Book Society was formed in 1910, and the first Herd Book, in 1911, listed 419 registrations.

Present status

Numbers are declining, largely owing to the improved milk yield often obtainable from first crosses. In 1971 there were estimated to be about 220 cows and 8 bulls, since when a further decline has occurred. There are only four distinct sire lines. Most of the cattle are scattered in small herds throughout the Shetland Isles, the only fair-sized herd being that of the Department of Agriculture at Inverness.

Description

The Shetland is a small, light breed, not unlike the Jersey in build but even smaller. When the breed first attracted the notice of agricultural writers it was said that even the best of the cows weighed no more than two or three hundredweight, with up to four hundredweight for the oxen, but the ordinary stock was even smaller. In his *Agriculture of the Northern Counties and Islands*, 1795, Sir John Sinclair stated that the cows were milked three times a day and gave only about a quart at each milking. The breed has now increased in size, perhaps through better feeding, breeding and husbandry, until the average weight is now around six to seven hundredweight. Two Friesian bulls exerted some influence on the breed from 1923 onwards.

All the cattle are now black-and-white, but earlier there were also duns, greys, reds and blues, with dun or dun-and-white probably the commonest. In the first volume of the Herd Book only 11 out of 39 bulls were black-and-white. All the other colours have now been eliminated by selection, perhaps as a result of observation of the improvement in milk yields from black-and-white crossbreds produced from the Friesians. The breed normally has up-curving horns.

As might be expected, the breed is very hardy.

Uses

Dual-purpose, for it was originally the only breed on the Shetlands. The milk yield is not high, though higher than the levels mentioned by Sinclair, but the milk is fairly rich, with a butterfat content of over 4%. The heifers start breeding young, often producing their first calf at two years or less. Steers fatten quickly and are good converters of food, even if this is of indifferent quality. Their beef is said to be unusually tender. Their chief recommendation is their ability to thrive on poor grazing. Steers sold in 1975 averaged 646.5 pounds per carcase at 28.3 months. They had wintered on silage and straw, without concentrates, and finished on poor grass.

South and Westland

A breed developed from several local types indigenous to south-west Norway, with occasional crossing with Ayrshire and Jersey bulls.

Present status

Declining and perhaps in danger of extinction, as the Norwegian Red breed takes over.

Description

Colour, usually brownish red but occasionally with some mottling. Generally polled, but a minority has small horns. Bulls weigh 1500 to 1750 pounds; cows, 900 to 1000 pounds.

Uses

Dual-purpose, but primarily dairy. Can average 10,000 pounds of milk per lactation at over 4% butterfat in a fair-sized herd. Surplus bulls and heifers make useful beef animals.

53

Swedish Mountain

An ancient breed apparently indigenous to the northern provinces of Sweden, and previously Norway and Finland as well, the Swedish Mountain cattle bear a significant resemblance to the rare British White breed. A few have been exported to Britain, to introduce new blood to the British Whites.

Present status

Decreasing in number, through competition with more productive breeds.

Description

Colour, white with black or red markings. Some are almost entirely white with black or red ears, eyelashes and tail. Others are literally sprinkled with black or red blotches; while others have an extensive large black or red patch on the side, leaving only the under-parts and a line along the back white. The breed is normally polled, with a high topknot.

The Swedish Mountain is a rather small animal, the bulls reaching a weight of 1000 to 1400 pounds, the cows, 700 to 900 pounds.

Uses

Developed primarily as a milk breed in an inhospitable mountain climate. Exceptionally hardy and said to be long-lived and fertile, but its milk production does not compare with that of the Friesian and Ayrshire.

Tarentaise,
or TARINE

A mountain breed from the old kingdom of Savoy, in south-eastern France. Very hardy and used to poor pickings.

Present status

Numbers are not high, but the breed seems in no immediate danger.

Description

Colour, light brownish-red, with no white. Size medium. Bulls weigh up to 2400 pounds; cows average about 1300 pounds. Horns in female, of medium size and up-curved; in male, short and straight.

Uses

Originally all-purpose and especially a draught animal. Now dual-purpose, but more are specializing in milk than in beef.

Telemark

A mountain breed developed from several local types of indigenous animals in Telemark, which is a county in central Norway.

Present status

Declining and probably in danger of extinction, as the Norwegian Red takes over.

Description

Distinguished by the ancient colour pattern of a white band along the spine ('finching'), with white tail, white underparts and sometimes white mottling on head and body. Basic colour, reddish brown. Horns, long and up-curved in cow; shorter but still up-curved in bull. Bulls weigh 1500 to 1900 pounds; cows, 900 to 1400 pounds.

Uses

Dual-purpose but primarily dairy. Can average well over 10,000 pounds of milk per lactation, and the surplus animals make useful carcasses. Development of its full potential has, however, never been undertaken.

55

Texas Longhorn

The first European explorers to visit America found no indigenous cattle there, but within a few years of Columbus's voyage cattle had arrived with the first Spanish settlers. Over the next three centuries more were brought over to the Spanish and Portuguese colonies, mostly, of course, from the mother countries. In due course, many of them escaped from domestication and ran wild, forming immense herds, but those which remained on haciendas were, in general, subject to little breeding control. Thus American types of cattle were evolved by natural selection and adaptation to the environment.

The actual types of cattle first imported into America are a matter for speculation, but it seems likely that Andalusian cattle, deriving their long horns from ancient Hamitic types indigenous to North Africa, were prominent. Long horned cattle were roaming wild in northern Mexico as early as the 1550s, and, although the first actual record of any crossing the Rio Grande is dated 1690, some were probably in Texas long before then. Texas was, of course, then part of Mexico.

When in the middle years of the nineteenth century, the tide of human settlement surged westwards across the prairies, these long-horned cattle of Texas were at hand to replace the almost exterminated bisons which had formerly grazed the grassy plains. Walter Baron von Richthofen, writing in the early 1880s, estimated that there were then 40 million cattle in Texas alone, in spite of the constant drain on supplies as more and more were driven off to populate the states to the north and west. At that time a North-western Texas Cattle-Raising Association had 223 members, several of whom possessed herds of more than 40,000 head, while no fewer than fourteen of them each owned 20,000 cattle. The total of cattle belonging to members of the Association was 1,400,000. Almost all of these would have been Longhorns.

Present status

Although exceptionally hardy and well adapted to the subtropical climate of Mexico and Texas, the Texas Longhorn could not match

56

the northern European breeds in efficiency of production, especially in beef. No sooner were the Longhorns established on the plains of the mid-West, therefore, than their 'improvement' by crossing with Shorthorns, Herefords, Devons and others began. Gradually these breeds took over, till by the 1920s pure Longhorns were difficult to find. In 1927 an attempt was made to rescue the survivors from oblivion. With a Congressional grant, more than 30,000 cattle showing Longhorn characteristics were inspected in southern Texas and northern Mexico, and from them 21, including one bull and one bull calf, were selected to start a foundation herd in the Wichita Mountains Wild Life Refuge at Cache, Oklahoma. Later, other herds were started, some on privately-owned ranches and some in parks and reserves, as at Fort Niobrara Game Preserve, Nebraska. The present total of Texas Longhorns in the U.S.A. is around 7,000. The breed should, however, be safe from extinction, being supported by the Texas Longhorn Breeders' Association (with headquarters at West Columbia, Texas), founded in 1964 and now having about 150 members.

Description

The original Texas Longhorns were lean, rangy cattle, well adapted to life on the arid ranges of northern Mexico and southern Texas. They had long bodies, flat sides, long legs, heavy fore-quarters and light hind-quarters. Their horns were in many instances immense; a span of four or five feet seems to have been normal, but in some of the older animals it extended to eight or nine feet. Colour very variable, with various patterns of white, red, black and tan, with white often predominant. Much speckling and brindling.

The Texas Longhorn is exceptionally hardy. It is a range animal, doing best when left to fend for itself in wild, unimproved country, where it can thrive on brush, cactus and other herbage of low nutritional value. The breed apparently owes little or nothing in its heredity to the English Longhorn, though, very far back, there may have been a common ancestry.

Uses

The Texas Longhorn was a beef animal, but not a very good one. It took a long time to mature, often six to ten years, and then a cow would weigh only about 650 to 750 pounds, a bull or steer up to 1000 or 1200 pounds. But this relatively poor performance depended, of course, largely on the level of nutrition and was part of the breed's compromise with its environment. It can do better under good conditions.

The breed has several notable advantages. Its long period of acclimatization in the sub-tropics made it highly resistant to tick-borne and other diseases. It produces small calves, thus reducing calving risks, but the calves grow quickly. Longevity is a feature of the Longhorn cow, which can go on producing an annual calf for up to twenty years. And the cows are good mothers.

There can be no doubt that the Longhorn has genes which could be of considerable value in revitalising the beef cattle stock of North America.

Tudanca

A breed of central Spain, north of Madrid.

Present status

Probably being maintained, though it could decline at any time.

Description

A small breed, the males averaging no more than 1000 pounds, the females about 750 pounds. Dark brown in colour, merging to black in the bulls. Horns, medium and curving upwards and outwards.

Uses

Traditionally all-purpose, with an emphasis in draught. Milking capacity poor, but the milk is very rich. Undeveloped so far.

Waldervieh,
or GERMAN FOREST CATTLE

An indigenous breed in the Black Forest of Germany.

Present status

There are two distinct types, each with its own well-maintained herd book. That found on the lower slopes of the hills is the *Vorderwälder*; that on the higher slopes, the *Hinterwälder*. Both types are low in numbers.

Description

Colour, reddish yellow, light red, brownish red or yellow, with white face, chest and underparts and often white flecks on the body. The Forest Cattle are lightly built, fine-boned animals of dairy type, *Vorderwälder* bulls weigh up to 1800 pounds, and the cows up to 1300 pounds. *Hinterwälder* animals are much lighter in weight, the bulls usually being no more than 1200 pounds and the cows as little as 700 to 800 pounds.

Uses

From draught animals these have been developed as dairy breeds. Their yields are low, averaging about 7700 pounds per lactation in the *Vorderwälder* and 5600 pounds per lactation in the *Hinterwälder,* both at around 4% butterfat, but, of course, they are small cows with low maintenance requirements.

Whitebred Shorthorn

Although there is a Whitebred Shorthorn Association, it exists primarily to ensure that there is a sufficient number of white Beef Shorthorn bulls to mate with Galloway cows to produce the popular 'Blue-greys' for northern fattening yards. The Whitebred Shorthorn can probably be correctly termed as a type within a breed. The cross can also be made the other way, with a Galloway bull on a Whitebred Shorthorn cow, but the use of the white bull is more usual.

White Park

Best known of the wild white or white park cattle of Britain is the Chillingham herd, which has been kept pure, without any introduction of blood from outside, for over seven hundred years. The herd is reputed to be descended from wild cattle which once roamed through the great Forest of Caledon. When Chillingham Park (in Northumberland) was enclosed by a stone wall in the year 1220 these cattle were trapped within its precincts, and there they still are, with access to 365 acres of rough grazing and woodland.

The same sequence of events has occurred in other corners of Britain, notably in Cadzow Park, Scotland, in Chartley Park, Staffordshire, and at Dynevor Castle, in south Wales. All the surviving cattle are much of the same type, though it is on record that the Chartley herd has experienced an introduction of Longhorn blood, and the Dynevor has been to some extent influenced by the Welsh Black. So prepotent are the wild white sires, however, that no visible evidence of these outcrosses now exists.

The origin of the wild white cattle is lost in antiquity. Their distant ancestor was probably the Aurochs, which once inhabited almost all the forest country of northern Europe. White cattle became involved in the religious cults of various peoples, naturally as animals for sacrifice. In France, and probably in Britain, Druids sacrificed white bulls under sacred oaks. But scholars have not yet decided whether the surviving British herds are directly descended from indigenous cattle or whether from white animals imported from Italy by the Romans.

From the eleventh century onwards chronicles refer from time to time to wild bulls, in some instances specifying white bulls with red ears. As late as 1526 Hector Boethe, the Scottish historian, writes of white bulls 'with crisp and curling manes, like fierce lions' in the Caledonian Forest. However, savage and intractable though these animals undoubtedly were, there is nothing to indicate how long their ancestors had run free. One has to take into account the widespread system of cattle-keeping in early and mediaeval Britain, whereby all the cattle of a village or settlement were under the charge of a cow-herd, who kept watch over them as they grazed on the common lands. In times of war and unrest there must have been many cattle which escaped into the forest and became wild.

In addition to the still surviving herds of wild white cattle, a number of others existed until comparatively recent times. In his *British Animals Extinct within Historic Times* J. E. Harting records herds once established at the following places:

Neworth Castle, Cumberland; Gisburn Park, Yorkshire; Somerford Park, Cheshire; Whalley Abbey, Lancashire; Wollaton Park, Nottingham; Leigh Court, Somerset; Woldenby Park, Northamptonshire; Barnard Castle, Durham; Bishop Auckland, Durham; Burton Constable, Yorkshire; Ewelme Park, Oxfordshire. In Scotland there were notable herds at Ardrossan, Ayrshire (destroyed in 1820); Blair Atholl, Perthshire (dispersed in 1834); Drumlanrig, Dumfriesshire (killed off in 1772); and Cumbernauld, Dumbartonshire (reputedly destroyed in 1570).

Present status

In May, 1977, the Chillingham herd numbered 48. Its numbers fluctuate, having fallen as low as 13 in April, 1947, after a severe winter in which all the younger animals, about twenty, perished. The ratio between males and females remains fairly constant, with three females to two males. Only one male, however, achieves dominance as the 'king' bull, and he alone serves the cows. He establishes this right by battle and retains it until he is defeated in single combat with a rival.

The Chillingham herd is completely wild. Even in polar weather they are reluctant to eat hay or straw spread out for them. Any calf that is handled by a human is usually killed when it rejoins the herd. In 1977 the herd was attacked by New Forest disease, which in some instances causes blindness, but treating the affected animals was impossible. Fortunately, the cattle have in the past proved resilient enough to take disease in their stride, and deaths from any diseases are very rare.

Of the other herds, the Chartley has moved to Suffolk, where it continues to flourish. It has supplied animals for the nucleus of new herds at the National Agricultural Centre at Stoneleigh, Warwickshire, and in the Cotswold Farm Park. The Dynevor herd is at present being served by the son of a Chartley sire. This bull has been put through his performance tests at the National Agricultural Centre, as have a number of cows in the Centre's new herd. Which is sufficient indication that they are by no means as wild as the Chillingham cattle. Vaynol Park, in North Wales, has also a herd, established in 1872, from Scottish animals, and these are nearest in type to the Chillingham cattle.

The Chillingham herd belongs to the Earl of Tankerville, on whose estate they live, but a Chillingham Wild Cattle Association, formed in 1939, helps with their maintenance. The animals are a tourist attraction and were visited by over 14,000 people in 1976. The visitors are naturally kept at a safe distance.

Description

Probably through having been inbred for so long, the Chillingham cattle are quite small. The cows average about 7 hundredweight liveweight; the bulls go to 10 hundredweight. They are white, with black eyes, dark lashes, dark brown muzzle, black hooves and black-tipped horns. The horns curve upwards and slightly inwards, more so in the cows than in the bulls. Some older bulls develop a mane and dark spots on the neck. Cattle of the other herds are similar, though in some the markings are reddish brown rather than black.

The polled British Whites are a distinct, commercial breed and are dealt with earlier.

Uses

The chief function of the wild white cattle at present is to serve as tourist attractions. The Chillingham herd in particular is of great interest to scientists, through having been kept pure and inbred for so many centuries. They offer, too, one of the few opportunities to study the behaviour and herd structure of cattle in the wild.

The commercial potential of the breed has hardly been explored. Attempts to cross some of the Chillingham cattle (which were removed from the herd and were not allowed back) with Shorthorns some years ago were not successful, owing to the unapproachable savagery of the progeny. Some of the more docile animals of the Chartley and other herds have, however, been investigated recently. A bull tested at Stoneleigh achieved an average gain in weight of 2.3 pounds per day and reached a weight of 1011 pounds in 400 days. Cows in the herd at the National Agricultural Centre at a recent weighing gave weights of from 1050 pounds to 1425 pounds.

Undoubtedly the wild white cattle have considerable disease resistance. They are also very hardy and are usually good mothers. In the Chillingham herd the average life of a cow is twelve to thirteen years, of a bull about ten years.

The semen of one bull, Royal Sultan, is available for A.I.

Sheep

Introduction

Wild sheep were indigenous to most of Europe and Asia and were undoubtedly among the earliest animals to be domesticated by Man. They are livestock which lend themselves readily to a nomadic regime and their domestication belongs to the pre-settlement period of human history. A considerable number of wild sheep species or types, confusing both in classification and nomenclature, has been described by zoologists. The two chief groups are the Mouflon (*Ovis musimon*) and the Urial (*Ovis orientalis*).

Archaeological evidence for sheep in connection with human sites begins about 5000BC in south-western Asia, and the earliest portrayal of sheep on the painted walls of Egypt dates from about the same time. In Egypt, however, the animals must have been alien introductions, for the sheep was not indigenous there. By the fourth millenium BC much crossbreeding was occurring, and established types, which probably deserve the status of breeds, were appearing.

They show tremendous variation. Some are hornless while others have multiple horns. In some the horns are curved in close to the face, like a giant ammonite shell; in others they are straight and horizontal, twisted into corkscrew shape. Some bear heavy fleeces, while others are clothed only in coarse hair. Many are apparently being kept chiefly as milk animals. The fat-tailed sheep of the Near East makes a very early appearance, as do those other eastern types with lop ears.

On the threshold of the Age of Improvement, in the mid-eighteenth century, Britain had innumerable local types of sheep, each bred over centuries to fit into local environments. The situation is hardly less complex today. In addition to well over forty recognised breeds there are in Britain a much greater range of crosses and double-crosses, and individual farmers are constantly experimenting with new ones.

Wensleydale sheep

Black Welsh Mountain

The Black Welsh Mountain breed has been evolved simply by selection for generations of black lambs born to Welsh Mountain ewes. The process has been going on for at least a century and perhaps much longer. Evidently there was always a small proportion of black progeny in the old Welsh Mountain flocks. The Flock Book dates from 1922.

Description

The breed is a compact hill sheep, distinguished most prominently by its short, thick, black wool. The impetus to develop the Black Welsh as a separate breed was probably provided by the quality of the wool, which in addition does not need dyeing. The head is short and wedge-shaped and is carried erect. The body is well rounded, with straight back and underline and is set on rather short legs. Only the males are horned. The tail is not normally docked. The skin is blue.

Present status

The breed has become so popular recently that it may not now qualify for inclusion as a rare one. The first investigations by the Rare Breeds Survival Trust revealed only thirteen flocks, comprising 312 animals in all, but this was soon corrected to about fifty flocks. One reason for the discrepancy was that the Black Welsh Mountain sheep had not all remained on their native mountains but had become dispersed throughout Great Britain, many of them being kept as park flocks in the demesnes of country houses, and many of these flocks were not registered with the Flock Book. By 1975 the number of registered flocks had increased to 135, and it was thought that there were still many more to be gathered in.

Overseas there are known flocks in Belgium, France and Germany, and also in Canada and the U.S.A.

The breed has not lost any of the hardiness acquired by life on the bleak Welsh hills and will fatten on quite poor pasture. Size, weight and fleece weight are increased when the animals are brought to rich lowland pastures. An asset of the Black Welsh Mountain breed is that, probably because of the colour, it is little affected by flies in summer.

Uses

Some flocks are undoubtedly kept partly for their decorative value, but as both meat and wool producers their performance is excellent. In 1973 Black Welsh Mountain sheep took both the championship and reserve championship for mountain breeds at the Royal Smithfield Show. The average lambing percentage is said to be 150, but selected flocks are averaging 200. The ewes are good mothers and have plenty of milk. The carcase weight averages 35 to 40 pounds, most of it of lean meat on a framework of light bones. Fleeces average about 4 pounds.

Cladore

There seems to be still some doubts about the validity of these sheep as a breed. They are a type of some antiquity found in very small numbers in County Galway. The name, an Irish one, means 'on the shore' and refers to the propensity of the sheep for getting much of their living from seaweed, like the North Ronaldshay breed. They appear to be related to the Galway breed and to the extinct Roscommon one.

Present status

A small group of Cladore sheep is being investigated by the Belclare Research Centre, in western Ireland. They are said to have been bred pure for at least fifty years. Whether any others exist is not known.

Description

This is a white, hornless breed (though some animals have coloured faces), carrying a fair amount of wool and a long tail. These hardy sheep have apparently been accustomed to subsisting largely on seaweed, picked up on the seashore.

Uses

A general purpose sheep. The ewes are good mothers and have plenty of milk.

Cotswold

The Cotswold is a breed of great antiquity, being probably descended from the sheep kept on the villa estates of the Cotswolds in Roman times. The mediaeval wool trade was founded on the fleeces of long-woolled sheep, many of them of Cotswold type and living on the high limestone downs of central England. Eighteenth century improvers took it in hand, increasing its size until it had become 'a gigantic sheep'. Its wool production was also improved, largely by crossing with the new Leicester breed.

It contributed extensively to the development of other breeds. The Oxford Down, for instance, derived from crosses between the Cotswold and the Hampshire Down. As early as 1484 Cotswold sheep were being exported to Spain, and in the nineteenth century considerable exports were made to Germany.

In England, however, the breed went into eclipse towards the end of the nineteenth century. Although first-class converters of food, they had tended to become over-large and coarse and to mature slowly. By the 1920s only a few flocks were left, and that the breed survived at all was due to the unflagging loyalty of a great old Cotswold flockmaster, William Garne.

Present status

The Cotswold has now emerged from its decades of obscurity. Although still low in

numbers, it is in no danger of extinction. The breed society had in 1977 26 members maintaining flocks, though not all the flocks were registered.

Description

A large, polled breed, with a prominent tuft of wool on the forehead. White-faced. Carries a heavy fleece, but the wool tends to be rather coarse.

The breed is hardy and does best on the high limestone hills from which it derives its name. On rich lowland pastures it still tends to become coarse.

Uses

Originally kept primarily for wool. Ewes give a clip of 10 to 15 pounds, rams up to 25 pounds. The old reproach of slow maturity has been eliminated, and the breed can now produce fat lambs of 40 pounds or more deadweight at eleven weeks. Cotswold rams are in strong demand for crossing with other breeds, such as the Clun and the Kerry Hill. It transmits its wool-producing potential to its progeny.

Dartmoor

Dartmoor

By the sixteenth or seventeenth centuries two main types of sheep lived on the moors and in the neighbouring valleys of Devonshire. One was a short-woolled animal, much like the unimproved Welsh Mountain and known as the West Country Mountain. The other was the Devonshire Nott, a polled breed derived apparently from a crossing of the Mountain sheep with some other type which carried more wool. In the eighteenth century further improvements on the Devonshire Nott were effected by extensive crossing with the new Leicester breed. From these crosses both the Dartmoor and the Devon Longwool were evolved.

Present status

In 1976 the Dartmoor Sheep Breeders' Association, which was founded in 1909, had 104 registered flocks, many of which had been kept pure for many years. Over 300 ram lambs and over 3000 ewe lambs were being registered annually. The breed would thus seem to be in no danger of extinction, but there is a threat to its separate identity through a suggestion to form an amalgamated group of long-woolled breeds in the South-west.

Description

This breed has a dense fleece of long, curled, lustre wool of fine quality. Size medium, with rather short legs. The rams are sometimes horned.

These sheep are used to ranging free on the cold, bleak moors of Devon and are therefore very hardy. They are seldom penned.

Uses

Fleeces average 17 pounds for a yearling ewe, 26 pounds for a yearling ram. The wool is used extensively in the manufacture of blankets. Dartmoor ewes when crossed with many other breeds produce excellent early lambs, which kill out at 40 to 48 pounds at 12 to 14 weeks. The lambing average is around 140%, and the ewes are good mothers and heavy milkers.

Galway

A breed, perhaps ancient, still surviving in comparatively small numbers in western Ireland. It seems to be related to the now extinct Roscommon breed.

Present status

Obscure. Some apparently pure representatives of the old Galway type still exist, but there is widespread crossing with other breeds, notably the imported Finnish Landrace in an attempt to create a new breed, the Fingalway.

Description

This is a white, long-woolled breed, of medium size, well covered with wool and resembling the Romney Marsh in appearance. Hornless.

As in other crosses, the introduction of the Finnish Landrace is being made with the purpose of increasing the lambing average,

which it does, but critics claim that the improvement is achieved at the expense of a lower fleece weight, lower growth weight and poorer lamb carcases.

Uses

All-purpose. In trials it has produced a fleece weighing 6½ pounds. The official lambing average is 140%. The lambs grow and fatten quite quickly.

Herdwick

To within the present century the Herdwick was one of the commoner hill breeds of northern England, and even now there are doubts about it being properly classified as rare. However, it is one of the older breeds which may decline quite suddenly and catastrophically and so is worth watching. Local tradition claims that the breed is descended from sheep which survived when ships of the Spanish Armada were wrecked on the Cumbrian coast, but their more likely origin is Scandinavian. The Herdwick Sheep Breeders' Association was formed in 1916.

Present status

More or less confined to the Lake District and its neighbourhood and probably declining in numbers. Projects have been launched in recent years to popularise its meat and also the excellent tweed and knitwear made from its wool.

Description

Medium-sized, with a thick fleece. Head bare and white. Legs short, with white feet. Rams are horned, ewes hornless. A rather remarkable feature of the Herdwick is that the fleece changes colour with age. In a young sheep at the time of the first shearing the fleece is very dark brown; in the next year it becomes light brown; and finally it changes to a pale fawn. All of these natural colours do not fade in fabrics woven from the wool. The wool often forms a mane, or ruff around the neck.

The breed has the reputation of being extremely hardy, its native home being harsh mountain slopes ranging to altitudes of over 3000 feet, in a high rainfall region. It has proved its ability to survive heavy snowfalls outdoors and has an impressive record of longevity.

Uses

T. L. Peacock's lines, 'The mountain sheep are sweeter, but the valley sheep are fatter,' could certainly apply to the Herdwick, which produces carcases of splendid succulent meat. The breed is perhaps best known, however, for its wool, which can be made into an excellent tweed. A home knitting industry using Herdwick wool for sweaters and other forms of winter knitwear, some of it for export, is developing in the Lake District.

Hill Radnor

This is an old breed on the upgrade. It is said to have originated from the indigenous tan-faced sheep of Wales and perhaps the West Country but has acquired the status of a pure breed only from 1949.

Present status

The breed is both increasing its numbers and extending its range.

Description

A lively mountain breed, with a good white fleece and light brown face and legs. Ewes are always hornless, but some of the rams carry horns. Although active, these sheep have a reputation for staying on the proper side of fences better than most mountain sheep.

The breed is very hardy but very adaptable.

Taken from its mountain pastures, where it thrives in bleak weather conditions, it adapts well to the richer grasslands of the lowlands and quickly puts on weight.

Uses

Pure Hill Radnors are efficient producers of both meat and wool. Fleeces from mountain ewes average about 4½ pounds of washed wool, from lowland ewes about 6½ pounds. The quality of the wool is high, making it suitable for tweeds and soft flannel. Under mountain conditions the lambing average is around 120%, on lowland pastures 165% or more. The ewes are outstandingly good mothers, with plenty of milk, and are often purchased by lowland farmers for mating with rams of other breeds.

Jacob

The antecedents of this striking piebald breed are obscure. The name refers to the sheep owned by the patriarch Jacob as recorded in the Book of Genesis, and some have imagined that the breed is directly descended from a type kept in the Middle East in those distant days. Unfortunately for that argument, the New English Bible translates the word to which the adjectives 'spotted and brindled' apply as 'goats' not 'sheep'!

Almost every possible country of origin has been suggested for them, including Syria, South Africa, Spain, Portugal, Persia, Morocco and Siberia. Predictably, one tradition has it that their progenitors were brought over, like so many other breeds of domestic animals, by the wrecked ships of the Spanish Armada. Apparently the term 'Jacob sheep' was first applied to one flock only, at Hampton Court, and was later extended to others of the same type. The latest evidence suggests that the piebald sheep of Britain had a common origin in a park flock somewhere in England before the

middle of the eighteenth century, and that is about as far as we can go at present.

Present status

For a couple of centuries or so Jacob sheep were mainly an ornamental breed kept in country parks and estates. A breed society was at last formed in 1969, since when the breed has gone from strength to strength. In 1975 it had more than 150 registered flocks, with a total in excess of 3000 sheep. Nearly all of the larger agricultural shows now have classes for the breed.

Description

The colour changes from black and white in young lambs to a dark rusty brown and white in adults. The proportion of black (or brown) to white varies, some individuals being almost entirely black, others white with only a few spots. Both sexes are usually horned, some of the animals carrying two, four or even six

70

horns, though there is a proportion of polled individuals. The sheep are alert, intelligent and rather slimly built, though the improved type tends to be heavier. Jacob sheep are adaptable and versatile and need no special treatment.

Uses

The Jacob is developing as two distinct types, one belonging to breeders who are content with it as an ornamental sheep, just as it is, while the other has been taken in hand by breeders bent on improving its commercial potential. The improved Jacob now has a body weight, in ewes, of over 130 pounds and produces a fleece with an average weight of around 4 to 6 pounds. Its wool is highly regarded, being soft and springy and with an attractive natural colour which does not fade. It is much in demand for fashioning fancy fabrics. The ewes are prolific and good mothers, with a lambing average of over 180%. They are often crossed with a ram of some downland breed to produce a quick-maturing early lamb. Jacob rams are often used on Dorset Horn ewes for the same purpose, or for further breeding, for the Jacob x Dorset ewe is an excellent mother.

Leicester Longwool

That the Leicester should have fallen to the status of a rare breed comes near to being incredible. This was the sheep breed on which Robert Bakewell concentrated his efforts in the second half of the eighteenth century. The new or improved Leicester which he created, using basic stock which he found in the Midlands together with crossing material from unknown sources, quickly spread to almost every part of Britain and was used to improve dozens of other breeds, particularly longwools. Leicester rams were also exported to virtually every sheep-producing country, making notable contributions to the sheep stock of France, Germany, Australia and New Zealand.

Bakewell's aim was a quick-fattening, mutton-producing animal, in which ambition he succeeded. In pursuit of his ideal, however, he sacrificed certain other qualities, including weight (though he deliberately kept his breed to a medium size) and quality of fleece. His new Leicesters certainly fattened easily, but on good rations they tended to become too fat. So, although in great demand for crossing with other breeds, as a pure breed they became none too popular.

Present status

The present-day Leicester has left the Midland pastures and is concentrated on the wold farms of East Yorkshire, where some of the leading flocks are kept on the old-style arable system. There are also numbers of Leicesters in New Zealand and Australia. The Leicester Sheep Breeders' Association was formed in 1893, with headquarters at Driffield, and there is also a breed Flock Book in Australia.

Description

The Leicester is a typical longwool, with a heavy fleece of curly, lustrous wool. Face and legs white, with ringlets of wool dangling over the forehead. The breed is a large, heavy one, shearling rams attaining weights of over 330 pounds, while one old ram tipped the scales at 472 pounds. The average fleece

Leicester Longwool

weight for ewes is 10 to 13 pounds, for yearling rams, 14 to 20 pounds.

Although originating on the fertile grassy plains of the Midlands and now concentrated on the arable farms of East Yorkshire, where it is often folded on swedes and other fodder crops, the Leicester is hardy, the climate of the Yorkshire Wolds being as austere and chilly in winter as that of any other corner of the British Isles.

Uses

The Leicester produces large, heavy lambs, the quality of whose meat has been greatly improved by modern breeders. The quality and weight of the wool have also been restored. Probably the greatest asset of the breed, however, is its propensity for producing first-class rams for crossing. Its rams are widely used on both down and hill breeds of sheep, the progeny being heavy, meaty and early maturing.

Lincoln Longwool

The Lincoln Longwool is, like the Cotswold, one of the venerable breeds of British sheep, having as its probable origins the sheep kept on Roman estates around Lindum (Lincoln) nearly two thousand years ago. From Lincolnshire it spread westwards into the Midlands and indeed to more distant parts of England, for there are references to Lincoln sheep in Wiltshire in the early thirteenth century. The wool from these sheep, known as Lindsey, played an important part in the great mediaeval wool trade of England. It seems that before Bakewell began his selective breeding programme which resulted in the creation of the new Leicester (for which see *Leicester Longwool*) the old Leicester breed was virtually indistinguishable from the Lincoln, and it is likely that Bakewell used the Lincoln extensively in his experiments.

Present status

In Britain the Lincoln Longwool is now more or less confined to the county of Lincolnshire and is relatively low in numbers. It has a breed association, formed in 1892. Outside Britain its status is not known, but the breed has been exported in considerable numbers to nearly all the world's sheep-breeding countries. An anonymous historian of the breed in 1938 stated:

> In thirty-seven years (1896-1932) more than 70,000 Lincoln sheep were exported to Australia, New Zealand, Canada, South Africa, Egypt, the Argentine and all other South American republics, the United States, Mexico, Russia, Spain, France, Germany, the Netherlands. The majority of the sheep were sent into these countries for crossing with the native breeds.

The celebrated Australian Corriedale was founded on crosses between English Long-wools (chiefly Lincolns) and Merino sheep, as also was the Australian Polwarth, which is approximately three-parts Merino to one-part Lincoln. America has several Lincoln-based breeds, of which the most notable is probably the Columbia, based on a Lincoln-Rambouillet cross. In Argentina many Lincolns have remained pure, and the breed is said to be still one of the most numerous in the country. On a global scale, therefore, the Lincoln is far from being a rare breed.

Description

The Lincoln is one of the largest sheep breeds, with a broad, deep body, fairly long legs and an erect carriage. It carries a heavy fleece of long, curly, lustre wool, the locks on its forehead hanging down in ringlets and often hiding its eyes. Face and ears are blue-grey.

The Lincolnshire countryside to which the Lincoln is native is exposed to cold north-east winds blowing in from the North Sea. There flocks have acclimatised themselves equally well to the bare hillsides, with their thin soils, and to the coastal marshes. In short, the Lincoln is very hardy and adaptable; as an additional asset, it is free from most diseases of the feet.

Uses

The Lincoln is noted for producing great quantities of both meat and wool. As a

butcher's animal, it is the practice to allow the lambs to grow on to the age of nine to twelve months, when they produce a carcase of 60 to 66 pounds deadweight. Mature animals can become far heavier, and there are records of ewes attaining weights of over 3½ cwt. The fleeces are similarly weighty, averaging perhaps 14 to 16 pounds, though with individual animals yielding much more. Young ewes will often give a clip of 25 pounds, while a shearing ram has been recorded as giving a fleece of 42 pounds. However, the main purpose for which Lincolns have become celebrated has been crossing with other breeds. Its popularity in Australia has been based on the fact that it matches particularly well with the Merino. As a sire the Lincoln ram will transmit not only the ability to produce weight in both body and fleece but also the lustrous quality of its wool as well as its splendid stamina.

Llanwenog

Llanwenog

The Llanwenog is a traditional breed in a district of south-west Wales, an inland area where the counties of Carmarthenshire and Cardiganshire meet. It is said to have been developed in the late nineteenth century from a black-faced flock in the village of Llanllwni, crossed with Shropshire rams.

Present status

Well established in its native district and now becoming quite popular in neighbouring areas. It is a sheep of the valleys rather than the high hills.

Description

In appearance and conformation the breed owes much to its Shropshire progenitors. It has a compact body, white fleece and black face, with a tuft of wool on the forehead. No horns.

Although not specifically mountain sheep the breed is hardy, thriving on both the meadow pastures and the hill slopes and summits of the Welsh valleys.

Uses

The breed is very prolific and has won many trophies for high lambing percentages. In the Wool Marketing Board's lambing competition in 1965 the Llanwenog triumphed over all other breeds with a lambing percentage of 230. The ewes are good mothers so are in demand for producing early fat lambs.

Lleyn

The Lleyn has been derived from the use of rams of two other breeds on the native mountain sheep of north-west Wales. At some time prior to the middle of the eighteenth century Roscommon rams from Ireland had been used on the local ewes. Towards the end of the eighteenth century rams from Bakewell's new improved Leicester breed were employed on the progeny of this earlier cross. The resultant breed remained well established in their secluded corner of Britain without attracting

74

much attention from outside until 1968, when a breed society was formed.

Present status

The formation of the breed society in 1968 found 10 flocks, comprising about 500 breeding ewes, in Anglesey and the Lleyn peninsula of Carnarvonshire. By 1977 the number of breeders had increased to 50, and some of the sheep were finding their way into other districts, including Ireland.

Description

The Lleyn is a hornless breed, entirely white and with a face free from wool. Medium size, with some variation. No special treatment required; the breed is reasonably hardy.

Uses

General purpose. Its lambing percentage is fairly high, averaging about 170. Most ewes have plenty of milk and are good mothers. The quality of the carcase is high, but the lambs do not as a rule have remarkable growth rates.

Lleyn

Manx Loghtan

The Manx Loghtan has been found on the Isle of Man from time immemorial, though even in the early nineteenth century it was low in numbers and confined to the poorer pastures on the hills. It is evidently related to a group of primitive multi-horned sheep of which examples have survived in St Kilda, Iceland, North Africa and, until quite recent times, the Shetlands. The Jacob sheep is also related, as are several four-horned types found in America.

Present status

By around 1950 the stock on the Isle of Man had dwindled to seven ewes and one ram. They were in the hands, however, of an enlightened breeder, Mr Jack Quine, who retrieved the breed from the threatened oblivion and who is still in charge of the largest flock, which is jointly owned by the National Trust and the Manx Museum. Altogether there may now be between 100 and 200 animals on the Isle of Man and about half that number in England, including a small flock at the National Agriculture Centre at Stoneleigh, Warwickshire. There is also said to be a small feral stock on the Calf of Man. The breed is now increasing and is in no danger.

Description

The name 'Loghtan' is derived from two Manx words meaning 'mouse-brown', which exactly describes the colour of the wool. There should be no trace of white on a pure Loghtan. Most rams have four horns, and females two, but the number of horns can vary from none to six. The tail is short. The Manx Loghtan is a smallish breed, about 85 pounds liveweight being the average for ewes.

Uses

Undoubtedly the Manx Loghtan was once an all-purpose breed adapted by long acclimatisation to life on the exposed uplands of its native island. It seems, however, that probably through inbreeding it lost some of its hardiness and mothering qualities. It is now recovering its stamina. Fleeces are not heavy but the wool is soft and demi-lustrous. The interest of the breed lies chiefly in its rarity, its primitive characteristics and its genetic possibilities.

Mayo Mountain

An old breed of western Ireland, somewhat similar to the Scottish Blackface, which was introduced around the beginning of the twentieth century to 'improve' the Mayo Mountain and finished by completely swamping it. The breed is now extinct.

A strain of the Scottish Blackface — the breed now found on Mayo Mountain.

Moorit Shetland

The name is confusing. 'Moorit' means reddish brown and is frequently used to describe a colour variety of the Shetland breed. But the Moorit Shetland is a distinct breed developed on the Castle Milk Estate in Dumfrieshire from unrevealed crosses, though Shetland and Soay blood may be suspected.

Present status

In 1975 a total of 14 ewes and seven rams were known, in two flocks, but a few others were believed to exist.

Description

A horned breed (in both sexes) with short, close wool of attractive reddish colour.

Uses

Its chief asset is its wool, which retains its natural colour when spun and woven, rendering dyeing unnecessary.

Norfolk Horn

Robert Trow-Smith (*A History of British Livestock Husbandry to 1700*) estimates from the statistics given in the Domesday Book that the sheep population of Norfolk in 1086 was around 90,000. They were probably of the old Norfolk Horned type, which even then had lived in East Anglia from time immemorial, for sheep skeletons from Grimes' Graves (Neolithic flint mines of c 2000 BC) reveal a very similar animal. Though much maligned by agricultural writers of the late eighteenth century (Arthur Young described it as an example of 'the usual wretched sorts found in England on poor soils'), it was still abundant at the start of the nineteenth century. Its doom was probably sealed by the widespread adoption of the Norfolk four-course system of husbandry, which involved growing root crops on which sheep were folded. Norfolk Horns were free-ranging animals able to get their living from the meagre grasslands of heaths, downs and marshes and apparently did not take kindly to hurdle pens, while other breeds gave a better performance under the new system. Throughout the nineteenth century the breed declined and by the beginning of the twentieth century only a few flocks remained. In 1959 the survivors were passed to the Zoological Society of London and domiciled at Whipsnade Zoo. There they stayed until 1968, when they were transferred to the National Agricultural Centre at Stoneleigh, Warwickshire. There were then 12 pure-breds (6 rams and 6 ewes) together with 8 cross-bred Suffolks.

Present status

Unfortunately, long inbreeding had left its mark. Such lambs as were born were sickly. Numbers dwindled further, and, despite all efforts at rescue, the old breed became extinct. However, recognising the approach of the inevitable, the N.A.C. and other breeders took steps to retain the genetic heritage of the Norfolk by crossing the last ram, who died in 1973, with Suffolk ewes. As a result, they now have rams which have seven-eighths and fifteen-sixteenths Norfolk blood, from which it is hoped to create a new version of the old breed. The Suffolks themselves are closely

related to the Norfolks, having originated from a chance cross between a Southdown ram and a Norfolk ewe.

Description

A rather long-legged, lanky sheep, with a heavy head and short, fine fleece. Horned in both sexes, the ram's horns being particularly well-developed. Face and legs black. Old pictures show some Norfolks with mottled fleeces. The breed was agile, nervous and difficult to confine.

The Norfolk Horns were used to living rough, finding their own living amid thickets, heaths and brambles, where their long legs served them well, but they adapted quite

readily to better conditions, except confinement.

Uses

Its hardiness and ability to thrive on meagre grazing enabled it to hold its position for many centuries. The lambs were slow to mature but produced succulent, tasty meat. The wool was not of the highest quality, and estimates of clips range from 2 pounds to 8 pounds. When moved to richer pastures, however, the Norfolk Horn could do much better in both wool and meat production. First crosses with other breeds were generally of high quality and abounding in hybrid vigour.

North Ronaldshay

Until recently this breed was confined to the island of North Ronaldshay, the northernmost of the Orkneys, where it had lived from time out of mind. It has a peculiar habitat. The island is entirely surrounded, above high tide mark, by a high drystone wall some twelve miles long, the prime purpose of which is to protect the cultivated land from the sheep, which live on the outside of it, on the foreshore. Nothing else being available in this strange environment, the sheep have adapted themselves to a diet of seaweed. They have become, indeed, quite selective, preferring kelp above all other species. The sheep are brought off the beaches to inland pastures for lambing, remaining there for about three months.

Present status

While the total sheep population of the island amounted to several thousand and so the breed seemed in no danger of extinction, it was felt that it was highly vulnerable to foot-and-mouth disease, an outbreak of which would have been followed by the slaughter of the entire flock. There was also a new hazard in North Sea oil, a slick of which could destroy the seaweed on which the sheep live. Accordingly in 1974 the Rare Breeds Survival Trust transferred about 180 animals to the neighbouring island of Linga Holm, which it had purchased for that purpose. By 1977 the Linga Holm population had more than trebled. At the same time smaller numbers were taken to other island homes, including the islet of Lihou, in the Channel Islands, and Pabbay, in the Hebrides. The breed is now much more widely distributed than ever it has been.

Description

A small white or grey sheep, horned in the males. A small proportion of lambs are grey brown or black, and an even smaller proportion moorit (reddish). On Linga Holm the ratio of black lambs has been high.

The North Ronaldshay breed is an outstanding example of adaptation to a particular environment. The seaweed diet produces strange adjustments in the physical make-up of the sheep. The iodine content of their milk is, for instance, very high, and the sheep also have the ability to utilise the copper content of their ration much more efficiently than most sheep can, with the result that when given a diet with a much reduced level of seaweed some have died of copper poisoning. These and other physiological phenomena are still being studied.

Uses

General purpose. Its interest lies in its ability to thrive on its remarkable diet.

Oxford Down

The Oxford Down was one of the later of the Down breeds evolved to meet the demand for good and early maturing lamb and mutton. The programme began in 1830, with the crossing of Hampshire Down rams (the Hampshire Down was itself a new breed) with Cotswold ewes, but proved to be a long one. The new breed was not exhibited at a major show until 1851, and its Flock Book was opened in 1889.

Present status

The Oxford Down never became very numerous, largely because its chief function was to produce rams for crossing with other breeds, and ram-breeding flocks, though highly important, do not need to be very large. The number of breeding ewes now living is estimated to be between 500 and 1000.

Description

This is the largest of all the Down breeds and among the largest of all sheep breeds in Britain. Adult ewes can weigh 200 pounds or more. The breed is heavily built and carries a dense white fleece, which extends to the legs and to a prominent topknot on the forehead. Face, ears and feet are blackish-brown.

The breed is not horned. Like other Down breeds, the Oxford has been bred for folding on arable fields, though it does quite well on good quality grass.

Uses

Oxford Down lambs are large, healthy and have a high growth rate. These qualities the ram transmits to its crossbred progeny. The breed's fortunes are therefore largely dependent on public taste. When large meaty animals are in fashion, the Oxford Down flourishes; when the public demands small joints, the breed goes into decline. It produces wool clips to match its size, a fleece of 10 pounds being a good average. Oxford Downs cross particularly well with the Scottish Half-bred.

80

Portland

In the eighteenth century a breed or type of sheep known as the South-western Horned or the Dorset was widespread in the south-western counties of England. Both the modern Dorset Horn and the now very rare Portland are probably descended from this stock. The breed takes its name from the rocky Isle of Portland, Dorset, where it formerly lived on the exposed, stonewalled pastures on the cliffs. However, it is only fair to mention that this is yet another breed said to have originated from stock brought over by the Spanish Armada. As none of the Spanish ships landed at Portland, the sheep are supposed to have escaped and swum ashore.

Present status

Though a small flock has now been re-introduced, the breed was extinct on Portland for many a long year. However, it did survive on a few farms scattered widely over the country, and these stocks have existed separately for so long that three distinct bloodlines have become established, which should be helpful to the future of the breed. In 1975 the Flock Book had 66 foundation ewes in 11 flocks, and a few others were known to exist. One flock is at the National Agricultural Centre, Stoneleigh, Warwickshire.

Description

The Portland is a rather small, greyish sheep, the lambs being much darker (even reddish-brown) at birth. Both sexes are horned, the ram's horns being often spectacularly spiralled. The breed is docile. Face and legs are greyish white.

This is a very hardy breed, accustomed originally to grazing on the sparse herbage on the windswept Isle of Portland. They can adapt themselves readily to better rations, however, and when treated as pets they become very tame.

Uses

General purpose. As with all small, light sheep, the meat is said to have a superlative flavour. One of the characteristics of the much more numerous Dorset Horn is the ability to produce three crops of lambs in two years, and some Portlands also have that capacity. Not all of them do, however, and breeders who have run rams continuously with ewes around the year have reported only one crop per year, in January. The incidence of twins is very low.

Roscommon

The Roscommon sheep was developed in western Ireland in the late eighteenth and early nineteenth centuries along the same lines as the new Leicester breed in England and indeed owed much to imported Leicester rams. It has been called *the* longwoolled sheep of Ireland. Earlier there may have been other importations of English sheep which, crossed with the smaller Irish native breeds, gave the Roscommon its size. In the late nineteenth century it was the dominant breed in Ireland, most of the million or so sheep found in the province of Connaught at the turn of the century being Roscommons. A breed society was formed in 1895.

Present status

Believed extinct. This remarkable reversal of

The Galway: the modern-day representative of the Roscommon.

fortune was brought about not so much through any notable deficiency in the Roscommon but through the introduction of other breeds for crossing with it. There are plenty of sheep about with Roscommon ancestry. At various times exports have been made to South America, New Zealand and Russia, and there may possibly be animals of pure stock surviving there.

Description

A large, longwoolled sheep. White face, ears and legs. Hornless. No tuft of wool as a forelock. A good, hardy breed, used to wind and rain.

Uses

General purpose. The wool was of excellent quality, and fleeces averaged about 10 pounds. The lambs, when marketed in late summer, were heavy and carried relatively little fat, but they were rather slow to mature, a characteristic which provided an incentive for bringing in other breeds for crossing.

Ryeland

An ancient breed, the Ryeland is claimed by some to be descended from sheep kept in the west Midlands in Roman times, nor is there anything inherently improbable in such a theory, though it cannot be proved. In the Middle Ages some of the best quality wool, on which commodity the commerce of England largely depended, came from a short-woolled sheep from the neighbourhood of Leominster, Herefordshire, and was widely famed as 'Lemster ore'. It is thought that the small breed which yielded this fine wool was 'improved' in the early nineteenth century by crossing with Bakewell's new Leicesters. The result was a larger and sturdier sheep of Down type, carrying more meat and producing early-maturing lambs, but the wool quality was lost.

Present status

Pure Ryeland ewes are now thought to number less than 1,000. The early home of the breed

and the district from which it takes its name was the 'rye-land' around Ross, in Herefordshire, and Herefordshire is still its headquarters. There would seem to be no immediate danger of extinction, for the rams are in considerable demand, and there is export trade.

St Kilda

Description

A white, hornless breed, neat, compact and straight-backed. Resembles the smaller Down breeds and, like them, has a thick, close fleece of short wool. Nose and feet are white. Wool covers most of the face and cheeks but leaves the nose and circles around the eyes bare. Hardy and adaptable. Docile and healthy.

Uses

A good general-purpose sheep, especially suited to arable farming. It is chiefly valued today as a sire for crossbred fat lambs, at which it excels. Overseas it is still much in demand for crossing with the Merino, for this same purpose. Also for introducing the poll factor into horned breeds.

St Kilda, or HEBRIDEAN

The name St Kilda is a misnomer. The breed found on the island group of St Kilda, 50 miles west of the Outer Hebrides, is the Soay (for which see *Soay*). A more apt name for the St Kilda is the Hebridean, which is now being officially adopted. Although originally confined to the Hebrides it was introduced at a relatively early date to certain private parks in England, where it is well established.

Present status

Now well distributed throughout Britain, though chiefly as an ornamental feature of private parks. A survey in 1974 revealed the existence of 450 to 500 breeding ewes, and numbers have probably increased rather than declined.

Description

A primitive breed, akin to the Manx Loghtan, the Soay and other breeds of the western fringes of Britain, the St Kilda is a small sheep with multiple horns, usually four. Agile, fine-boned and rather long-legged. Colour of both wool and face, black or dark brown.

Very hardy. Does well on rough grazing and, indeed, seems to prefer weeds to good grass.

Uses

The breed's commercial potential has been hardly explored. The fleece is fairly long, up to 6 inches, and averages 3 to 3½ pounds. The sheep are lightweight, ewes averaging no more than about 85 pounds live, but they cross satisfactorily with rams of the long-woolled or Down breeds and produce good lambs. Lambing average is usually about 130% but under good conditions can be much higher.

Shetland

This is the indigenous breed of the Shetland Isles but has been much modified by the use of mainland Scottish breeds, introduced to increase the size. A breed society was formed in 1926 to attempt to preserve the ancient qualities of the breed.

Present status

There are still many sheep on Shetland, and most of them are of this breed or crosses with it, but the crossbreds probably outnumber the purebreds. Retaining adequate numbers of pure animals is still a problem.

Description

One of the smallest of British breeds (hence the incentive to cross with bigger rams). Mostly white woolled with white faces, but there is a small proportion of moorit (reddish) sheep, and some flocks of these colour-marked animals have been established. Rams horned; ewes hornless.

As might be expected from a breed with such an austere homeland, the Shetland is extremely hardy and does well on rough pastures.

Uses

The Shetland produces wool of superb quality, which is plucked rather than shorn. Knitted garments of Shetland wool are world famous. The quality of the meat is excellent, but the carcases are small. First-cross and second-cross lambs, notably with Cheviots and the Down breeds, are a good economic proposition.

Shropshire

The foundation of the Shropshire breed is to be sought in the crossing of the improved sheep breeds of the late eighteenth century, notably the improved South Down, with the indigenous sheep of the heaths and moors on the borders of Shropshire and Staffordshire. The native sheep were a mixed lot, of varying types, and it is not known which played the most prominent part in the creation of the new breed. In the second half of the nineteenth century and the early decades of the twentieth the Shropshire was very popular. It was the first breed to be represented by a Flock Book Society, formed in 1882, and large numbers were exported to almost every sheep-producing country in the world, especially America.

Present status

In the second half of the twentieth century the fortunes of the breed declined, and a survey in 1975 indicated the existence of less than 500 breeding ewes. Since then the Shropshires have gained some popularity and now seem in no danger of extinction.

Description

The Shropshire is a typical, handsome Down sheep and is often known as the Shropshire Down. Medium size, with a fairly heavy and dense fleece of short wool. Ears, face, nose, eye spectacles and legs are black, but wool covers the poll and much of the face.

Highly adaptable and capable of thriving on either grass or arable. Robust and hardy.

Uses

General purpose. Produces quick-maturing early fat lamb, with meat of excellent flavour. Lambs can be ready for slaughter at from 9 to 11 weeks. 8 to 10 pounds is an average weight for a fleece, with rams producing fleeces of up to 18 pounds. The prime purpose for which Shropshires are bred, however, is for crossing with other breeds, to produce early lambs. Their downfall came about through relying too heavily on the export trade in rams, in the course of which breeders tended to emphasise certain characteristics, such as fat tails and woolly topknots, which were popular in America but not in Britain. When the American market collapsed, largely because of a foot-and-mouth disease epidemic in England, breeders found it impossible to recover much of their lost British trade. Modern breeders have now had plenty of time to iron out unwanted features, and the breed is once again on the upgrade.

Soay

The Soay is the native breed of sheep of the islet of Soay, one of the tiny St Kilda group in the Atlantic some 50 miles west of the Outer Hebrides. After the human inhabitants with their livestock had been removed from Hirta, the largest and only inhabited island of the group, in 1930, 107 of the Soay sheep were transferred to Hirta, where they multiplied rapidly.

Present status

There are thought to be between 1000 and 1500 Soay sheep on Hirta. In addition, sheep from Hirta have been taken to mainland Britain, where, in 1975, there were an estimated 650 breeding ewes in 1975.

Description

A primitive breed of sheep related to the wild Mouflon of Corsica. Predominant colour, dark brown to black, with a proportion (about 10% to 20%) of lighter animals. The dark sheep also usually have lighter underparts and a lighter rump. Horned. Very hardy indeed. Good for grazing poor land.

Uses

The commercial possibilities of the breed have not been fully explored. Lambing average is around 120% but can be considerably higher under favourable conditions. The breed is a light one, with ewes averaging only 55 to 60 pounds, and the lambs grow relatively slowly. The wool is short and close.

Southdown

To an older generation of farmers, of whom I am one, it seems strange to be including the Southdown as a rare breed. I remember it as one of the most popular breeds in southern England. It is also one of the oldest, deriving from a light, freckled-faced type of downland sheep which was indigenous to Sussex and neighbouring counties before the eighteenth century improvers started work on them. The breeder who took the old Southdowns in hand was John Ellman, of Glynde, Sussex, who began operations in about 1780, though precisely which breeds he used is uncertain. Pictures of some of his sheep survive, but even they are so different from the modern Southdown that we can only guess at what the original type was like before he started his improvements. Ellman was exhibiting his Southdown sheep in 1798, but it was not until 1897 that the Southdown Sheep Society was formed. The breed was in high favour for the intervening century and was used to improve most of the Down breeds. As well as being popular in Britain, the Southdown was exported in large numbers to nearly all of the world's major sheep-producing countries.

Present status

A survey in 1975 revealed a total of 1510 breeding ewes in 56 registered flocks. It was only in Britain that its numbers were low, however. New Zealand at the same time could muster 82,022 breeding ewes, and there were very large numbers, too, in Australia and France, among other countries.

Description

A short-legged, compact rather small Down breed. Its physiognomy is unmistakable, the head being broad between the ears and the face short, rather pointed and mouse-coloured. A dense fleece of white, fine-textured wool. Hornless. Versatile, adapting to either arable or grassland husbandry.

Uses

The Southdown has been a victim of fashion. It catered between the wars for the trade in lightweight carcases with small joints, a market on which New Zealand in particular based its export trade. Wartime and subsequent conditions demanded larger and heavier carcases, and the Southdown tended to fall out of favour. However, the surviving flocks of Southdowns are mostly of the larger types, though the early maturing qualities are still retained, and the quality of the meat remains high. Southdown fleeces average from 4½ to 8 pounds for ewes and tegs, 7 to 12 pounds for rams. The quality of the wool is topgrade among Down breeds.

Teeswater

In the early eighteenth century, before the beginning of the great age of livestock improvement, the Teeswater was a very large, coarse, longwoolled breed allied to the Lincoln and found in Teesdale, on upland pastures between Durham and Yorkshire. It was known locally as the Yorkshire Mug. One of the first breeds to be crossed extensively with Bakewell's Leicester, it was reduced in consequence in size and prolificacy, even though its carcase was improved, and as a result lost its popularity. A cross which produced the Wensleydale helped to retrieve it from threatened extinction, and a small stock survived in upper Teesdale.

Present status

The remaining flocks were brought together into a Flock Book in 1949. Since then the breed has improved its status and is becoming more widely known. It has considerable importance as one of the basic breeds used in producing the very popular Masham of northern England (the formula is often: Teeswater x Swaledale = Masham).

Description

Still a large, longwoolled sheep, with long-stapled, curly, lustre wool. Body broad and deep, carriage erect. Face and feet, mottled. Hornless. Very versatile. Rears twin lambs

economically and without traditional concentrate feeding.

Uses

Bred primarily to supply rams for crossing with ewes of hill breeds. The quality the sires transmit to their progeny are prolificacy, early maturity, carcases with a high ratio of lean meat, fleeces of high grades and good mothering ability.

Welsh Badger-faced

The Badger-faced or Torddu sheep is a colour variation which has from time out of mind occurred in the Welsh Mountain sheep of north Cardiganshire.

Wensleydale

Present status

A 'Torddu-Badger-faced Welsh Mountain Sheep Society' was formed in the autumn of 1976. The exact status of the breed is still being established.

Description

This is a typical Welsh Mountain sheep with face markings, of longitudinal black and white stripes, almost exactly similar to those of a badger. The word 'torddu', meaning 'black belly', refers to the fact that the wool on the belly is black, in contrast to the whitish-brown fleece that covers the rest of the body.

Uses

As for Welsh Mountain sheep.

The Wensleydale had its origins in 1838 when a large ram of the new Leicester breed was mated with some Teeswater ewes or possibly with ewes of the now extinct Yorkshire Longwool. One of the progeny was an outstanding ram, known as 'Blue Cap' because of the deep blue colour of his skin, a characteristic which he transmitted to his progeny and hence to the whole Wensleydale breed. Founded in Yorkshire, the Wensleydale soon spread to all the neighbouring counties and to some farther afield. Exports were made to a number of countries, including the West Indies and France. In the latter country the descendants of nineteenth century imports developed into the Bleu du Maine breed, specimens of which have in recent years been brought back to England. A Flock Book was opened in 1890.

Present status

Numbers have declined alarmingly in Britain. A 1975 survey showed 231 ewes in 23 flocks. The situation has since improved a little, and there are numbers of Wensleydales, though to what extent they are pure is unknown, in other countries.

Description

A large, upstanding, longwoolled sheep. The fleece is long (12-inch staple), lustrous and curly, with ringlets hanging over the face. Body broad and deep. Face, blue. Hornless.

The pure Wensleydale is an arable sheep, fattening well on turnips and swedes. It is hardy.

Uses

The prime purpose for which the Wensleydale is bred is for producing rams for crossing with ewes of the hill breeds, notably the Swaledale. The Masham, highly popular in northern England, is the progeny of either a Wensleydale or a Teeswater ram on Swaledale ewes. Its status as a ram-producing breed rather as one to be valued for its own pure qualities is probably the chief reason for its low numbers. Nevertheless its performance in its own right is impressive. Its fleece averages 14 pounds and is some of the best lustre wool in the world. It produces lambs with a rapid growth rate and weighty carcase (80 pounds or so

dressed weight). The ewes are prolific, with a lambing average of about 200%, and are good, milky mothers.

The blue pigmentation of the skin has proved an asset in tropical countries, such as Africa and the West Indies, to which numbers of Wensleydale rams have been exported. The blue coloration is, however, not a completely true characteristic; about 15% of the lambs in pure flocks are born black and are rejected for registration. A smaller proportion are too light in colour and are likewise rejected.

White-faced Dartmoor

Before breeds as we know them became established several types of medium long-woolled sheep roamed the moors of Devon. The longwool characteristic seems to have originated from the introduction of old Leicester sheep to the horned mountain ewes of Welsh Mountain type that were indigenous. The White-faced Dartmoor represents one of

White-faced Dartmoor

White-faced Woodland

the oldest types of moorland sheep, with the influence of introduced breeds less than in some other Devon breeds.

Present status

A Flock Book has only recently been formed but is providing a nucleus for evidently quite numerous White-faced Dartmoor breeders who have kept their sheep pure for years.

Description

A medium-sized, sturdy sheep. White head, face, feet and fleece; nose black, and occasionally black spots on ears. Rams horned; ewes hornless. Very hardy, living on open moors at high altitudes for most of the year.

Uses

General purpose. Average weight of fleece, 10 to 16 pounds, though higher under favourable conditions. Lambs produce carcases (45 to 60 pounds deadweight) of good lean meat. Ewes are good mothers and have plenty of milk. Excellent for crossing with Down breeds.

White-faced Woodland

The Whitefaced Woodland has its headquarters in Woodland Dale, a Pennine valley on the borders of Yorkshire and Derbyshire, and probably about 90% of animals in the breed live within the radius of a few miles. An alternative name is the Penistone, after the market town at which most sheep of the breed change hands, but recently there has been a suggestion that the Whitefaced Woodland and the Penistone may be two distinct breeds. The breed is undoubtedly founded on the coarse, black-faced, heavy-horned Linton type of mountain sheep, which inhabited the southern Pennines at the beginning of the eighteenth century. Later in that century there was some crossing with the new Leicesters and other improved types, and early in the nineteenth century the Duke of Devonshire imported Merinoes which had a considerable influence in the formation of this breed.

91

Present status

Hardly a rare breed, for there are believed to be upwards of 3000 breeding animals. However, the concentration of such a large proportion of them in such a small area makes the breed particularly vulnerable to an epidemic, as of foot-and-mouth disease. In recent years new flocks have been established in other districts.

Description

One of the largest of the hill breeds. Upstanding, rather long-legged, white-fleeced, with white face and legs and a pink nose (a Merino legacy). Horned in both sexes.

Versatile and adaptable. Commonly run as a hill sheep but adapts well to more luxurious conditions. Perhaps not quite as hardy as some of the mountain breeds.

Uses

General purpose. In its native territory the Whitefaced Woodland is used to produce heavy lambs with a daily liveweight gain of nearly one pound. Lambing average is from 160% to 200%, and the ewes are milky and good mothers. Apart from their performance as purebreds, however, the Whitefaced Woodlands are in demand for crossing with other hill breeds, the rams being used to put size and weight into the progeny from lighter types.

Wicklow

A breed apparently indigenous in the Wicklow Mountains of Ireland.

Present status

Probably extinct

Description

Apparently very similar to the Welsh Mountain. Hornless. A hardy hill breed.

Uses

Noted for producing very early lambs.

Wiltshire Horn

Unimproved Wiltshire Horns were an indigenous type, once found in great numbers on the chalk downs of Wiltshire and adjacent counties. The story of their decline makes interesting reading.

At the beginning of the nineteenth century there were reckoned to be at least half a million ewes grazing on Salisbury Plain alone. Forty years later, only a few flocks were left. By the end of the century, all had disappeared and even the memory of them had been lost. The Wiltshire shepherds interviewed by W. H. Hudson in the early 1900s, while collecting material for his classic *A Shepherd's Life*, knew nothing of them and were puzzled by the quantities of sheep's horns they discovered in old wells, for in their experience only an occasional ram had horns.

The dramatic disappearance of the Wiltshire Horns was due entirely to unwise 'improvement'. At the beginning of the period the breed was certainly good material for improvement. It had a poor, scraggy carcase, was of ungainly appearance, with horns too large for its head and head too large for its body, and

it produced next to no wool. When the improvers had finished with it, it was a vastly better animal; the only snag was that it had lost its ability to thrive on the meagre pickings of the high chalk downs.

It was rescued from extinction by a handful of breeders in Buckinghamshire and Northamptonshire, who, being on the 'Drovers' Road' from North Wales to London, stocked rams for the drovers to take back to North Wales. At the same time, certain breeders in Caernarvonshire, finding the supply of rams drying up, also took the precaution of establishing ram-breeding flocks of their own. For the Wiltshire Horn rams were much favoured for crossing with Welsh Mountain ewes for producing early lambs.

Present status

The breed still survives on a few farms in the South Midlands and in North Wales, and perhaps in a few other places as well. One small flock has, indeed, returned to its native Wiltshire. Numbers are, however, very low.

Description

A rather large sheep, remarkable in that it grows no wool worth speaking of but has its body covered with a mat of dense hair. Both sexes are horned, the horns of the ram being massive and spiralled.

The quality of grazing having vastly improved since the Wiltshire Horns were banished from Salisbury Plain, the breed will now thrive on any normal grassland.

Uses

Having no inclination to grow a fleece, the Wiltshire Horn concentrates on producing meat. This it does rapidly and efficiently. Lambs are normally ready for market at 3 months. Lambing average — from 100 to 150%. As a rule, only ram-breeding flocks breed pure Wiltshire Horns. Most rams are mated with ewes of other breeds, especially the Welsh ones, for producing quick-maturing lambs. Lambs from this cross are often shorn before marketing and will yield a useful fleece of 4 to 5 pounds.

93

Pigs

Modern pigs of Iron Age type

Introduction

The eternal complaint of pig farmers is that pigs are either 'muck or money'. Markets tend to oscillate between glut and scarcity. The problem arises from the fact that it is so quick and easy to react to market vagaries. Cows normally produce one calf per year, ewes no more than two or at the most three lambs, but a good sow will supply two litters each of from ten to fourteen pigs in the same period.

For the same reason, the rise and fall of breed fortunes tend to be equally rapid. When a breed is popular it can quickly achieve an impressive strength of numbers. That happened with the Gloucester Old Spots in the 1920s. But its success proved its own undoing, for breeders were tempted to use as many animals as possible for reproduction, including stock which would have been better slaughtered. As a result, performance began to decline and the breed went out of favour.

Pig fecundity, of course, works in the other direction as well. An outstanding boar can make a much wider and quicker impact on a breed than can a good bull or ram. Several stories are advanced to account for the red colour of the Tamworth, but all agree in attributing it to only one boar, which is a perfectly feasible explanation.

Domestic pigs are descended from a group of wild pig species whose habitats extend across Eurasia. Their domestication probably

began in Neolithic times, coinciding with the formation of the first permanent human settlements. Neolithic tribesmen settling down to farming would draw their first stock from the wild pigs roaming in the neighbouring forests. Probably, therefore, modern pigs have descended from a wide range of primitive types.

European pigs were an unprepossessing lot in the Middle Ages. Early illustrations depict them as lean, ugly, long-snouted, bristle-backed scavengers, rooting for their living in woods and farmyards in the country and in middens and rubbish heaps in the towns. By the early eighteenth century regional types had begun to be recognised, their quality depending very much on their diet. In cheese-making districts they fared quite well on whey; in other places beans were grown for fattening them.

Major improvements really started with the importation of Chinese pigs, the earliest of which appeared in Britain in the 1770s. In their native country these had already been subjected to many centuries of modification and had developed broad backs, short snouts, short legs and a propensity for fattening rapidly. Although probably evolved from a different species of wild pig, they interbred rapidly with European stock and immensely improved it. Neapolitan pigs, too, are frequently mentioned in English records. They also were of Chinese origin but had spent an intervening period in Italy.

LEFT   Berkshire pigs

Berkshire

At one time, towards the end of the eighteenth century, a breed known as the Berkshire was dominant over the greater part of Britain. It was not, however, a pig exactly like the modern Berkshire but was a red-and-black pig, without the snub nose or 'dished' face which is now a feature of the breed, and with lop ears instead of the prick ears which now distinguish it. It was, on the other hand, small-boned, short-legged and inclined to fat, which gave it an advantage over many of the other unimproved types of pig then existing. It obviously owed these characteristics largely to the Chinese and Neapolitan pigs introduced in the second half of the eighteenth century.

By the early years of the nineteenth century frequent crossing with these types was refining the Berkshire to something near its present type. Size was reduced and fleshing qualities improved. By the end of the century the Berkshire was a specialist pork pig of the best type, sharing the market with the Middle White. Breed society was formed 1885.

Present status

The breed suffered badly in the shift to the bacon market, in which pork tends to be a by-product of the bacon pig, which is slaughtered prematurely when the price happens to be right. The Berkshire survives, but in small numbers. In the nineteenth century extensive exports were made to the U.S.A., Australia, New Zealand, South Africa, Argentina and Japan, and recently, in 1976, three Berkshire boars were imported to Britain from Australia to reinforce the British stock.

Description

The Berkshire is the typical pork pig — short-bodied, full-fleshed, short in the leg, 'dished' face, fine bones. Its colour today is black, often with white on the legs and face. The ears are now erect, not lop. The Australian type is a rather longer and leaner animal than the British. The breed repays comfortable housing and adequate feeding.

Uses

Although first crosses with larger breeds will produce passable bacon carcases, the Berkshire is better kept entirely as a porker, at which it excels. The young grow and fatten quickly, reaching a weight of 100 pounds in 17 to 18 weeks. The sows, docile and good mothers, are moderately prolific.

British Lop

This breed was formerly known as the National Long White Lop-eared, and its ancestors as the Cornish Lop-eared and Devon Lop-eared. It is also related to the Ulster White, the Cumberland and the Lincolnshire Curly-coat. Evidently it represents an ancient type, doubtless improved by crossing with imported stock (Chinese or Neapolitan). It survived chiefly on small Devon and Cornish farms, particularly in the neighbourhood of Tavistock, and has had a breed society since about 1918.

Present Status

Still reasonably well established in Devon, Cornwall and adjacent counties, with some expansion into the Midlands, but little known outside its circle of breeders. The distance of its homeland from major centres results in its absence from most of the large shows.

Description

A white pig, with very prominent lop ears. Originally it was one of the largest British breeds but has been somewhat defined by crossing with other breeds.

Uses

Primarily a bacon pig, either as a purebred or crossed with Large White or Landrace. But it also grows fast and so is quite satisfactory as a porker. It is usually kept by small farmers who have little time for specialization.

The lop ears prevent the pig from seeing well, and in consequence it is easy to keep within bounds, besides being very docile. It is hardy and resistant to disease. On the farms of its native counties it is often put out to graze, with little housing.

Cumberland

An old-established breed once found through-out north-eastern England and the border counties of Scotland. A herd book was formed in 1916. The Cumberland is closely related to the Welsh.

Present status

The breed is rare but probably still survives.

Description

A large, white pig. The older type at least had large, pendulous ears, like the Cornish Lop-eared. Early nineteenth century writers said that Cumberlands would attain a huge size, feeding to 25 to 30 stone (350 to 420 pounds).

Uses

Reputed to be very prolific and excellent for crossing with the Large White for producing bacon pigs.

Dorset Black

Robert Trow-Smith, in his *A History of British Livestock Husbandry, 1700-1900*, gives the following account of the foundation of the Dorset Black. He says that about 1860 a farmer of Blandford, Dorset, mated two black 'Tonkey' sows with a Chinese boar and then crossed their progeny with a Neapolitan boar. About the same time another farmer in the same county conducted a somewhat similar experiment, though perhaps not with the same foundation stock; and the combination of the two groups developed and stabilised a breed which achieved some popularity in the late nineteenth century as the Dorset Black, or Black Dorset. The breed was also known as 'Coate's breed', after one of the founders. The 'Tonkey' sows mentioned were a breed from south-east Asia, deriving their name from Tonkin, which were introduced to Britain

perhaps in the eighteenth century but quite possibly in the seventeenth. The Chinese pig apparently arrived during the same period, as did the Neapolitan, which was an Italian cross between the Chinese and the local Italian pigs.

Present status

The breed is probably extinct.

Description

The Dorset Black was said to have been 'short, round and black'. Other writers describe it as a pig with a soft, blueish skin and fine-boned.

Uses

It was reputed to fatten readily but to become excessively fat, with very little lean meat.

Gloucester Old Spot

A white breed of pig with black spots or patches seems to have been widespread in the west Midlands until about the middle of the nineteenth century. The Gloucester Old Spot, also known as the Orchard Pig because of its propensity for fattening in autumn on fallen apples in the orchards of the West, has been developed from the survivors. Its breed society was established in 1914, and the breed reached the height of its popularity in 1921, when the society had no fewer than 1200 members.

Present Status

The breed is not immediately threatened with extinction but is low in numbers, with only 62 females registered in one recent year (1974). It is largely confined to the lower Severn valley.

Description

A large, lop-eared pig with a fairly thick coat. Colour—white with a rather sparse sprinkling of dark spots.

Uses

Primarily a bacon pig, capable of producing carcases, which are especially suitable for the heavy hog trade, on a scavenging diet. There has been a good deal of crossing with the Large White, Welsh and Landrace to produce the best type of carcase. The sows are prolific and excellent mothers.

The Gloucester Old Spot was bred for outdoor life, rooting for its living in orchards and woodlands and fattening on scraps and by-products (whey, etc.) of the dairy industry.

Large Black

Black pigs used to be widespread in East Anglia and in Devon and Cornwall and is said to have been developed as a distinct breed early in the nineteenth century. Its conformation and its black coat it probably owes, in a large part, to Neapolitan ancestry. Its breed society was established in 1899, and in the early years of the present century the breed enjoyed wide popularity, not only in Britain but in South Africa and South America.

Present Status

Not clearly defined, but numbers are probably low. The breed lost ground when the market demand developed for a white animal of standard carcase type. Before that the 'blue' pigs, resulting from a cross between a Large White boar and a Large Black sow, were very popular.

Description

Large, black and lop-eared. It has a long back suitable for a bacon carcase.

Uses

All-purpose. Its colour has been against it in recent years, but when 'blue' pigs were in fashion it was highly valued for the prolificacy and excellent mothering qualities of the sows. I was greatly impressed by the docility and litter records of a small herd of Large Black sows I once possessed.

The lop ears ensure that it is a good grazing animal, easy to keep within bounds because of the restriction on its field of vision. It forages contentedly. The black pigmentation of its skin makes it a satisfactory breed in tropical countries.

100

Lincolnshire
Curly-coat

A local breed developed in Lincolnshire as an all-purpose pig but used primarily as a baconer.

Present status

Unknown, but rare if not extinct.

Description

A large white pig with thick, curly coat. Lop-eared. Hardy.

Uses

A coarse pig, capable of reaching very heavy weights, though also capable of quick growth with an adequate diet.

Middle White

The bristly, scavenging pigs of the Middle Ages were vastly improved by the introduction of the fatter, sleeker Chinese pigs (some of which came via Naples and were known as Neapolitan) in the latter years of the eighteenth century. The Middle White is one of the surviving breeds which allows marked Chinese characteristics. In the middle of the nineteenth century Joseph Tuley, a Yorkshire breeder, laid the foundations of the Large White. A little later he crossed some of his Large White sows with a Small White boar and from the progeny developed the Middle Whites, which soon became popular.

Present status

The Middle Whites flourished throughout the late Victorian era and into the middle years of the present century. Then they suffered an eclipse. They are essentially a pork breed, and, with the demand growing for bacon, it became customary to slaughter immature bacon pigs to supply the pork market. The breed is now kept alive by a small number of loyal breeders, against the time when public demand will again make the keeping of specialist pork pigs economic.

Description and Uses

The Middle White has a snub-nosed or 'dished' face, like the Berkshire, a reminder of its Chinese ancestry. It is a superb pork pig, capable of growing very quickly and producing a much higher proportion of flesh to bone at an early age than do most of the bacon breeds. Its killing weight of 80 to 100 pounds carcase weight can be attained in 100 to 120 days. Killing-out percentages are good. Breeders

claim that the breed is disease resistant and very prolific. Figures compiled when the popularity of the Middle White was at its peak showed an average of 9.73 piglets born per litter and 7.49 reared.

The breed responds well to comfortable conditions and adequate rations. The animals are easy to keep within bounds, being disinclined to root and very docile.

Oxford Sandy and Black

See illustration overleaf

There is some doubt about the authenticity of this breed. Pigs of these colours have been found on Midland farms for centuries, but any cross between the Tamworth and the Berkshire will produce pigs of the same colours. It is claimed, however, that the original Sandy and Black had lop ears, while the Tamworth/Berkshire cross does not. One theory attributes the origin of the breed to a Dr Tustian who in the eighteenth century crossed a Gloucester Old Spot with a Tamworth and then the progeny with a Berkshire.

Present status

The breed is said to have been down to two herds in 1963. In 1975 there were at least fourteen breeders, but it would be interesting to know the antecedents of some of the animals.

Description

The basic colours are sandy-red and black, but there is considerable variation in the pattern. Generally the sandy-red is the base colour, with spots or splashes or larger areas of black. They are similar to the Tamworth in conformation. Hardy.

Uses

A good smallholder's pig and therefore all-purpose. It is said to grow and fatten quickly but to produce rather small litters.

Oxford Sandy and Black

Orkney

This breed, which was apparently found in the Orkneys, Shetlands and Hebrides up to at least the first half of the nineteenth century, was said to be no larger than a 'good-sized terrier'. It lived in herds, finding its own living around the crofts on the moors. Contemporary descriptions speak of it as a little monster, savage and voracious.

Present status Presumably extinct.

Description

Evidently it resembled a miniature wild boar, with long, erect bristles and a very strong and well-developed snout. The colour was generally brindled, and the ears stood erect and sharp-pointed. The breed was exceptionally hardy and thrifty.

Uses

Normally the Orkney, fending for itself, carried little flesh, but when brought to the farmstead and fed, even with a meagre diet of potatoes and scraps, it put on flesh very quickly, and its meat was of good quality. There was a considerable trade in supplying the carcases of these little pigs to ships. It is said that the longer bristles or hairs were woven into ropes for use in collecting birds' eggs from precipitous cliffs, the ropes so made being very much stronger than hempen ropes.

104

Tamworth

The origin of the Tamworth is obscure. A sandy-red and black type of pig was widely distributed throughout much of midland England in the second half of the eighteenth century but is referred to by contemporary writers as the Berkshire (see p. 96), which is even said to have been the local breed of Staffordshire, the homeland of the Tamworth. The separate development of the Tamworth and Berkshire seems to have started early in the nineteenth century, the chief factor in the change being the considerable use of Chinese and Neapolitan blood in 'improving' the Berkshire but not the Tamworth.

Some controversy has occurred over the origin of the golden-red or foxy-red colour that distinguishes the Tamworth. The story most widely accepted is that early in the nineteenth century a Sir Francis Lawley, of Middleton Hall, Tamworth, Staffordshire, received as a present from India a young red jungle boar. In 1814 he gave this boar to an employee who was leaving him to set up farming on his own, and in the succeeding years it was widely used by neighbours. The red colour would indeed be likely to be dominant in the progeny.

Another theory gives the credit to a red boar imported from Barbados to the village of Axford, near Marlborough, Wiltshire, about a hundred years earlier than Sir Francis

Lawley's importation. Yet a third account ascribes the red colouring to a boar brought from Ireland to Sir Robert Peel's estate, near Tamworth, in 1812. It seems quite possible that this last story has become confused with the first one, for the date is about the same, Sir Robert Peel and Sir Francis Lawley were near neighbours, and, finally, there is no other information about any red pigs being resident in Ireland at that period.

By the middle of the nineteenth century the Tamworth was well established and widely known, with classes at the most important agricultural shows. Its Herd Book was formed in 1885, and the breed was one of the founder members of the National Pig Breeders' Association's Herd Book in 1882. A large export trade developed, particularly to Canada, U.S.A., Australia and New Zealand.

Present Status

The breed is now uncommon in Britain. Perhaps not really rare but in sufficiently low numbers for three Tamworth boars to be imported recently from Australia to reinforce it. It is still found in considerable strength in Australia, U.S.A. and Canada, though the numbers are probably declining.

Description

A largish, long-snouted breed, remarkable for its golden-red colour. Prick-eared.

Uses

The Tamworth was bred as an all-purpose pig and is highly adaptable. It is regarded as a good producer of lean bacon carcases. The chief criticism usually directed against it is low litter size, but this is not necessarily a dominant feature of the breed and is being corrected in some of the leading herds. Some individuals are slow at reaching maturity but, on the other hand, thrive on indifferent rations. It is a good crossing pig, for use with white breeds.

Ulster White

A breed very similar to the Large White, once common in Northern Ireland. Its first Herd Book was established in 1909.

Present status

Now probably submerged by the Large White, through interbreeding. Good for both pork and bacon, but particularly bacon.

Description

Very similar to the Large White.

Poultry ————————————

Introduction

The wild ancestor of the domestic fowl is undoubtedly the Red Jungle Fowl (*Gallus gallus*) which is indigenous throughout India and Indo-China. Three other nearly allied species are found in the same region and may perhaps be considered races of the Red Jungle Fowl, as they are able to interbreed. Archaeological evidence suggests that the fowl was fully domesticated in India by about 2000 BC. A painting in the tomb of the Pharaoh Tutankhamon proves that it was known in Egypt in about 1350 BC, but it did not become generally distributed around the eastern Mediterranean until about the eighth century BC. By the time of Aristophanes (c 400 BC) practically every Athenian household possessed poultry.

The purpose for which the domestic fowl was first prized is unknown. The emphasis in the earliest documentary references, in the Hindu sacred literature, seems to be on the cock's courage and prowess and on his usefulness in heralding the dawn. He must have been a valuable timekeeper in the days before clocks. Some early civilizations had a prejudice against eating a cock's flesh, while in others cocks were an acceptable religious sacrifice.

It is safe to say that well before the Christian era domestic poultry were commonly kept throughout the ancient world, including north-western Europe outside the bounds of the Roman Empire, and were valued for their flesh, their eggs, their prowess as fighting birds, their religious significance, including their role as a symbol of fertility and virility, and also for divination, and finally, time-keeping.

The natural colours of the Red Jungle Fowl are red with black wings and tail, a pattern found with modifications in many modern breeds. In the first century BC hens of this coloration were, according to the Roman poet Columella, the best layers, but birds exhibiting other colour patterns were obviously in existence. Centuries earlier the Egyptian god Anubis required the sacrifice of white cocks, while other deities demanded black ones.

By the early seventeenth century, when documentary evidence for the various types of poultry begins, we can recognise what may now be referred to as breeds established in certain localities. Thus the Scots Dumpies were described in 1678, at which date similar poultry were known in France and Germany. The Campine was known in Belgium, the Hamburgh in Yorkshire and the Redcap in Derbyshire from at least that time. Indeed, most countries and regions, from Spain to China, had their own specialities.

In the nineteenth century the scientific use of this very varied material to create new breeds gained momentum. Early in the century new types were introduced to Europe and America from India and the Far East, and from them and the older indigenous stock new breeds were evolved. Breeders in the U.S.A. were particularly active, establishing such sub-

Brahma cock

sequently popular breeds as the Rhode Island Red, Plymouth Rock and Wyandotte.

As specialisation was pushed still further, the demand increased for auto-sexing breeds, in which the sex of a newly-hatched chick is evident from the difference in the colour of the down. Thus when a Rhode Island Red cock is mated with a Light Sussex hen the cockerel chicks have silvery white down, like their dam, while the pullets have golden-brown down, like their sire. From the mating of a brown or black cockerel, such as a Black Leghorn, with a barred hen, such as a Barred Rock, the male chicks will be readily identifiable by a light greyish patch on the head. Auto-sexing makes it possible to eliminate unwanted cockerels at birth, thus economising in food and space.

For a time these straight crosses served the industry well, but now the process has become further sophisticated. The big international poultry empires each has its own carefully prepared and secret formulae for breeding the types of bird which suit it best, whether for egg-laying or table. These super-birds are labelled with trade rather than breed names and are intended primarily for mass production systems.

The keeping of pure-bred stock has thus become the province of the smaller breeder. The specialist giants obviously have an interest in maintaining a basic stock of the breeds from which their synthetic types are fashioned. Other breeds of no direct interest to any

specialist at the moment are kept alive by small groups of enthusiasts and fanciers. They are the potential stock for future developments and represent a genetic bank which it would be unwise to squander.

In Britain the affairs of the poultry world have been organised and administered by The Poultry Club since its formation in 1877. One of its main concerns has been to establish standards for the various breeds.

Affiliated to The Poultry Club are specialist breed clubs, each concerned with one breed. Currently these clubs number between forty and fifty.

In 1969 The Rare Breeds Society was formed to cater for those breeds which had no specialist society. This Society has since been very active and has created such interest that new specialist societies have been formed for several breeds formerly included in the 'rare' category. At the time of writing these are the Dorking, Brahma, Cochin and Araucana. Our list of rare breeds included in this book does not necessarily conform with the official list of breeds under the wing of the Rare Breeds Society, for some of those which have specialist societies or clubs are decidely uncommon.

Ancona

A breed of Italian origin, first imported into Britain in the 1850s. Rosecomb Anconas were introduced in about 1900.

Description

A light breed. Many colour varieties, the commonest of which is black, shot with green and speckled with white. Large, erect, deeply serrated comb, erect in cock, falling to one side in hen. Lobes, white. Legs, yellow spotted with black. There is also a rosecomb variety. Weights, male, 6 to 6½ pounds; female, 5 to 5½ pounds.

Uses

A good layer of large white eggs. Although small carries a good, meaty breast. Males often crossed with females of heavier breeds, notably Rhode Island Reds.

Andalusian

A breed of Spanish origin, introduced to Britain about 1850 and considerably developed there. Much used in the development of other varieties.

Description

A light breed. Colour, blue, the feathers edged with black. Black hackles and, in males, wing coverts. Tail luxuriant and flowing. Comb erect and deeply serrated in male; falls in one fold in female. Lobes, white. Legs and feet, slate colour or black. Beak, slate colour or horn. Weights — male, 7 to 8 pounds; female 5 to 6 pounds.

Uses

Lays very large white eggs.

Appenzeller Spitzhauben

A small breed, about midway between a fowl and a bantam, originating in Switzerland.

Description

A light breed, of Minorca or Hamburgh type but smaller. Has an unusually-shaped crest, pointing forward, and a V-shaped comb, like small horns. Colour, silver-white, spangled with black.

Uses Primarily kept for show purposes.

Araucana

A light breed of Chilean origin, taking its name from the Arauco district of southern Chile.

Description

The commonest type has blue-grey or lavender plumage, but there are also brown, black, red, golden, cuckoo and pied colour variations. In the blue-grey variety the feathers are edged with a darker grey. This breed has a topknot of feathers, more flowing in the male than in the female, and only a small comb. Legs, blue-grey (or colour of the plumage). Beak, black. Erect carriage. A rather small breed, with shorter legs than those of most of the light breeds. Weight — males about 6 pounds; females, 5 pounds.

Uses

The chief distinction of the Araucana is that it lays blue or green eggs.

109

Ardennes

An old-established breed in the Ardennes district of eastern Belgium, where it was traditionally kept on free range and did not take kindly to penning.

Description

Evidently has some Game blood in its ancestry. Colours, typical red-and-black pattern (red on upperparts, black on underparts and tail) in male; female, partridge or light brown. Weights — male, 5 to 6 pounds; female, 4 to 5 pounds.

Uses

Dual-purpose; a good table bird and fairly good layer (eggs white). Very hardy.

Aseel

A game breed, reputed to be derived from the fighting cocks of India. The name is said to be a corruption of 'asl', meaning pure or high-caste.

Description

A broad-breasted, robust breed of typical game conformation. Colours various. One of the commonest is the Spangled, which is a blending of white, black and brown. There are also light red, dark red, white, black, blue, yellow and grey colour varieties. Comb, pea-type. Legs, yellow, in most varieties.

Uses

Generally regarded as a fancier's breed, though with useful table qualities.

Augsburger

A German breed, developed in the Augsburg region in the 1880s.

Description

A breed with concave, bow-shaped comb characteristic of the Sicilian Buttercup. Colour — black. Weights — male, 7 to 8 pounds; female, 6 to 7 pounds.

Uses

Mainly a fancier's breed but dual-purpose.

Australorp

Also known as the *Black Orpington*, under which name it originated in England in the 1880s. From exports to Australia the breed was further developed as egg-laying specialists and was later brought back to England in the 1920s, under its new name.

Description

A dual-purpose breed, of Orpington or Sussex type. Black, shot with green, is the only colour. Comb, single, upright and medium-sized. Comb, lobes and wattles, red. Legs, black. Weights — male, 8 pounds; female, 7 pounds.

Uses

Good for both table and eggs. Fattens readily. Very docile and easy to keep within bounds. In Australia the breed achieved egg-laying records, but it could not bring a matching performance with it to Britain, probably on account of the different climate. Eggs rather small.

Barbezieux

A breed developed in France, probably from Black Minorca foundations.

Description

A light breed, graceful and elegant in appearance. Colour, black with greenish sheen. Comb, single, serrated and erect in male; drooping in female. Lobes, white. Weights — male, 7 to 8 pounds; female, 6 to 7 pounds.

Uses

Primarily for laying large white eggs.

Barnevelder

The breed takes its name from Barneveld, in Holland. Introduced to Britain in 1921, where it became very popular for a time.

Description

A dual-purpose breed of the Rhode Island Red type. Colour, laced black and red, the black being shot with green. There are also several other colours, including partridge,

black, silver and white. Legs, yellow. Comb, red, single, erect and well serrated. Beak, yellow with dark tip. Eyes, orange. Weights — male, 7 to 8 pounds; female, 6 to 7 pounds.

Uses

Owed its popularity largely to its rich brown eggs. Flesh of good quality and quantity on culled hens and cockerels. Not excessively broody.

Belgian Game

The Belgian version of the Game fowl.

Description

In general appearance resembles the Malay Game but has a straighter back and a more erect tail. Comb — triple. Colours — the red-and-black game pattern, the females being mostly black, with golden hackles. Weights — male, 11 pounds; female, 9 pounds.

Uses

Kept mainly for show purposes but a useful table bird.

112

Blue Madras Game

A Game breed of Indian origin, probably nearly related to the Indian Game. A few were introduced to Britain about the beginning of the twentieth century but never became popular, though it is thought to have been used in the development of some other blue breeds. Little is known about the breed, but apparently it did not always breed true to colour.

Bourbourg

A French breed.

Description

A heavy, well-shaped bird, with erect stance, broad breast and back and rather short legs. Colour, white with green-black tail and black stripes on hackles. Legs, cream-white and slightly feathered. Whiskery feathers around face. Comb, single, erect and serrated. Weights — male, 9 to 10 pounds; female, 7 to 8 pounds.

Uses

Dual-purpose but primarily table.

Brahma

A heavy breed, originating in India and introduced to the U.S.A. in 1850, to Britain in 1853. Said to derive its name from the river Brahmaputra. The breed experienced considerable development after becoming established in England and America and was largely responsible for the rapid growth, in the second half of the nineteenth century, of interest in fancy poultry.

Description

Large, heavy, stately birds, with erect posture. A notable feature is the heavy feathering on

the legs — a fan-shaped arrangement of feathers which sweeps the ground. There are two colour types, dark and light. The light is mainly white, with black-striped hackles and leg feathers and black tail and primary feathers. Pea-type comb, wattles and lobes, all red. Legs yellow. In the dark variety the plumage of the male is mostly black shot with green, though wing secondaries and back are white. Hackles and wing-coverts striped black-and-white. The female of the dark variety is, apart from a white head, almost entirely covered with dark feathers margined with white. Weights — male, 10 to 12 pounds; females, 7 to 9 pounds.

Uses

A good table bird but of interest mainly for showing.

Brakel

A breed developed in Belgium and Germany.

Description

A light breed, similar to the Campine, which doubtless contributed to its breeding. As with the Campine, there are Silver and Gold colour varieties, but on the back the barring is replaced by a solid silver or gold colour. Both single and rose combs are permissible. Lobes, white. Legs, slate-blue. Weights — male, 6 to 7 pounds; female, 5 to 6 pounds.

Uses

Kept primarily for show purposes, but dual-purpose, though with the emphasis on egg-laying.

Breda

A Dutch breed, widespread and formerly popular in the Netherlands.

Description

Fairly large fowl of barnyard type. Colour varieties — black, white, barred and blue. Weights — male, 7 to 9 pounds; female, 5 to 7 pounds.

Uses

Dual-purpose. Has old qualities of hardiness and thriftiness but rather slow maturity. Eggs, large. Fattens well when full-grown.

Bresse

A light breed, developed in southern and eastern France. Introduced to Britain in 1894, when it enjoyed a fairly short period of popularity and was widely used for crossing with the Rhode Island Red, Light Sussex and other heavy breeds.

Description

Not unlike the White Leghorn in appearance but rather stockier and heavier. Comb similar to that of White Leghorn but not so heavy. Colour (of the commonest variety), white, with white or pale blue lobes, pale blue beak, dark eyes, and slate-blue legs. There is also a

Campine

Campine

This breed is said to have been known in Belgium in the time of the Emperor Charles V (sixteenth century) and to have been introduced into Britain by the Huguenots. With such an ancient lineage it has provided foundation stock for more than one modern breed. In the present century it has been used (with the Barred Rock) to produce the auto-sexing Cambar.

Description

A light breed, of Leghorn or Minorca type. There are two main colour varieties, the Silver and the Gold. The Silver has a white head and neck but is otherwise barred white and greenish black. The Gold has a golden head and neck, the rest of its plumage being barred red and gold. Both single and rose combs are permissible, though the former is the commoner. Lobes, white. Legs, slate-blue. Weights — male, 6 pounds; female, 5 pounds.

Uses

Dual-purpose, though primarily kept for eggs. Early maturity, the pullets starting to lay when five or six months old. Plump-breasted and therefore a useful table bird, though small. Often used in the petit poussin trade. Non-broody and hardy, but can fly well.

black variety, with a dark beak; also, rare grey and blue varieties.

Uses

Although a light breed, the Bresse has been bred and developed primarily as a table bird and has a fleshy, meaty breast. It is quite a good layer, though the eggs of some strains tend to be small. Longevity, good.

Buff Medway

A breed developed around the turn of the century by a Mr Morton, of Gillingham, Kent. Thought to have been bred from Faverolles and Orpington parents. Never very popular or numerous. Probably extinct.

Description

Similar to an Orpington in build but otherwise nearly resembles the Faverolles, with characteristic muffles and feathered legs. Colour — golden buff. Comb, single, erect and serrated. Weights — male, 8 to 10 pounds; female, 7 to 8 pounds.

Uses

Dual-purpose. A very useful table bird, but also quite a good layer of brown eggs.

Castilian

An old-established breed in Spain, very similar to the Minorca.

Description

A light breed, compact and sleek. Chief colour is black, but there are also white and blue types. Comb, single, erect, serrated and rather large in male; drooping in female. Lobes, white. Weights — male 6 to 7 pounds; female, 5 to 6 pounds.

Uses

Primarily a laying breed, the eggs being large and white. Hardy but rather slow in maturing.

Chanticler

A breed of Canadian origin, introduced in the 1920s. Little information available.

Description

A light breed, white in colour.

Uses Primarily a laying breed.

White Cochin cock

Cochin

A huge bird, very heavily feathered, the Cochin is supposed to have originated in China, the first specimens being sent to Britain in 1843, as presents to Queen Victoria. It was subsequently much developed by British breeders.

Description

This massive bird holds itself very erect and is covered with great soft cushions of feathers which seem to be arranged balloon-like around its frame. Even the legs are smothered in feathers. There are several colour varieties, the commonest and the first to be introduced being the buff. The colour is even over the whole plumage. Comb, wattles and lobes, red; and the comb is single, erect and small. Beak and legs, yellow. Other colours are black,

Blue Cochin cock

white, cuckoo, partridge and blue. Weights — male, 10 to 13 pounds; female, 9 to 11 pounds.

Uses

Apart from its role as a fancy breed for shows, the Cochin is primarily a table bird, though some of its utilitarian qualities have been lost.

Columbian Rock

A breed developed in America from the Plymouth Rock crossed with the Columbian Wyandotte and the Light Sussex.

Description

A heavy breed. White with hackles edged with black and with black tails and wing primaries. Legs, yellow. Weights — male, 8 to 10 pounds, female, 6 to 7 pounds.

Uses Dual-purpose.

Coucou de Rennes

A French breed very similar to the Plymouth Rock.

Description

A massive breed, with deep body and broad breast. Colour, barred as in the Plymouth Rock, but the distinction lies in the colour of the feet, legs and beaks, which are white. Comb, erect, serrated and single. Weights — male, 8 to 10 pounds; female, 6 to 8 pounds.

Uses Primarily a table bird.

Courtes-pattes ———

An old French breed; the name means 'short feet'.

Description

A very short-legged breed, similar to the Scots Dumpie but not nearly so heavy. Body deep and very long. Colour, green-black. Comb, serrated, single and erect. Lobes, white. Tail, long and flowing. There is usually a tuft of feather beneath the beak. Weights — male, 4 to 5 pounds; female, 3 to 4 pounds.

Uses

Primarily a table breed, in spite of the small size; white fleshed and plump. Moderate performance as layers. Matures quickly under favourable conditions.

Coveney White

A synthetic breed evolved by a private breeder and accepted as pure in 1924. It is little known. Probably extinct.

Description

A light breed resembling the White Leghorn in most respects but having a bowl-shaped comb, serrated around the edges.

Uses Reputed to be an excellent layer.

Creve-coeur

A French breed, not unlike the Houdan.

Description

A medium to small breed, though the British version is considerably larger than the French. Like the Houdan it has a feathery mop top-knot and a peculiar forked comb which is, in fact, a double V-shaped comb. The colour is black, with green iridescence.

Uses

Dual-purpose, though with only a fair performance in each respect. Rather delicate.

Croad Langshan

This breed is said to have originated in Langshan, China, Major Croad being the man who first introduced it to Britain, in 1872. Considerably developed after its introduction, and used also in the development of other breeds.

Description

A large, heavy breed, rather similar to the Australorp. The commonest colour is a green-shot black, free from any other hue. Comb, wattles and lobes, red; beak, horn-coloured; legs, blue-black. The comb is upright, single, serrated and rather small. The legs are moderately feathered. There is also a less common white variety. Weights — males, 9 to 10 pounds; females, 7 pounds.

Uses

Dual-purpose. Has an excellent, meaty table carcase. Also noted for its brown and plum-coloured eggs, a characteristic which it transmits in crossing with other breeds. Hardy, docile and easy to keep penned. It usually comes into lay fairly late in the season and carries on laying until well into the winter.

Deutsche Langshan
or GERMAN LANGSHAN

A fairly recent German breed.

Description

Similar to the Modern Langshan but without the feathering on feet, the absence accentuating the length of the long legs. Black, with a green sheen, is the usual colour, but there are also white and blue-laced-with-black varieties. Weights — male, 10 pounds; female, 8 pounds.

Uses

A heavy table breed.

Dominique

Developed in America in the early years of the twentieth century.

Description

A barred bird, of Plymouth Rock type and coloration. Rose comb. Legs yellow.

Uses

Dual-purpose, but classified as a light breed.

119

Dorking

Dorking

One of the oldest of breeds, said to have descended from poultry brought to Britain by the Romans. Has probably contributed to a number of other breeds.

Description

A heavy breed, with several colour varieties. The oldest and probably the most numerous is the red, in which the male has bright red upperparts and glossy black underparts and tail, while the hen is reddish-brown, with black edging to each feather. In the silver grey, the red of the red variety is replaced by silvery white, while the hen has silver-grey plumage with dark edgings and with a salmon-red breast. There are cuckoo, white and dark varieties. Most varieties have a single, erect comb, but some have a rose-comb. Legs, white, shaded with pink. The Dorking has five toes on each foot. Weight — male, 10 to 14 pounds; females, 8 to 10 pounds.

Uses

Primarily a table breed.

120

Du Mans

The French counterpart of the Black Minorca.

Description

A light, elegant, compact breed, with plump breast, long back and flowing tail. Colour, glossy black. Legs and eyes, dark; lobes white. Differs from the Minorca in having a rose comb. Weights — male, 7 to 8 pounds; female, 6 to 7 pounds.

Uses

Primarily a laying breed, though has useful table characteristics.

Du Mantes

A French breed.

Description

Somewhat similar to the Houdan, but considerably larger and heavier. It also lacks the characteristic Houdan crest but has the tufts of fine feathers which are usually described as muffs and beard. Colour, black and white mottled, as in Houdan. Comb, single. Legs and beak, white. Weights — male, 7 to 9 pounds; female, 6 to 8 pounds.

Uses

Dual-purpose. Both table and laying qualities are good.

Exmoor

A modern breed established in 1950. Foundation stock consisted of Norfolk Grey, Houdan and Andulasian.

Description

The basic colour of this breed is blue, with upperparts of the male silver-white, the hackles being streaked with blue; breast feathers in both male and female laced with silver-white. Legs, black or purple-black; eyes, dark. Comb, single, with small tuft at rear; inclined to droop a little. Weights — male, 7 pounds; female, 5 to 5½ pounds.

Uses A dual-purpose breed.

Faverolle

A synthetic breed created in France in the second half of the nineteenth century and introduced to Britain in 1886, where it experienced further development. Breeds involved in its evolution were Cochin, Brahma, Dorking and Houdan.

Description

A densely-feathered breed, with thick plumage, feathered legs and puffs of feathers around the cheeks and beneath the beak. A deep and rather heavily built bird, with erect carriage. There are several colour varieties. The white is pure white; the ermine has black tail and black-streaked hackles as in the Light Sussex; the salmon is multi-coloured, with much black in the male; the black has a glossy greenish-black plumage. There are also blue and buff varieties. Upright, single comb; white legs and beak. Weights — male, 8 to 10 pounds; female, 6½ to 8½ pounds.

Uses

Dual-purpose, but especially good as table bird. Has been used quite extensively in recent years for developing new crosses or synthetic breeds for broiler work.

Frizzle

A breed of some antiquity, for it was known in the early seventeenth century. Probably originated in east Asia, though accounts of its country of origin differ.

Description

The chief peculiarity of the Frizzle is that its feathers curl 'the wrong way', making it look as though they have been brushed up. There are at least a dozen colour varieties. Comb single. Legs, varying in colour according to the colour variety. Weights — male, 8 pounds; female, 6 pounds.

Uses

Mainly a fancy breed, but can be a useful dual-purpose bird.

Gatenais

A French breed developed in the early twentieth century.

Description

A medium breed, with sturdy compact body, similar to the Plymouth Rock in build. Colour, pure white; legs, feet and beak also white. Comb, single, erect and serrated but rather small. Weights — male, 7 to 8 pounds; female, 6 to 7 pounds.

Uses Dual-purpose, and good in both respects.

Golden Essex

A twentieth century breed, with a lot of Golden Wyandotte blood. Probably extinct.

Description

Of Wyandotte type, with rather short legs, fairly long neck and short tail. Colour, reddish gold, with some black lacing; tail black in male. Legs, beak and eyes, yellow. Comb,

Hamburgh

single, erect, serrated and of medium size. Weights — male, 7 pounds; female, 5 pounds.

Uses Dual-purpose.

Known at the end of the sixteenth century and may have had a Mediterranean origin. Bred in northern England for more than two centuries; once very popular there and commonly exhibited at village poultry shows. Considerably developed by northern breeders and used in the evolution of many other breeds.

Description

A light breed, of Leghorn type. Compact, sprightly and neatly streamlined. The rose comb, though square in front, is tapered to a point and is worn like a crest. Lobes, white; legs and feet, grey-blue; eyes, red; beak, dark horn. Tail, long and luxuriant. There are several colour varieties, notably the Silver-spangled, Gold-spangled, Silver-pencilled, Gold-pencilled and Black. Weights — male, 5 pounds; female, 4 pounds.

Uses

Good layers.

Hornet

An old English breed, centred on Yorkshire, where it was once popular. Probably extinct.

Description

The name is derived from the comb, which, as in the La Fleche, is bifurcated, resembling a pair of horns. The males have a crest or top-knot and a long, flowing tail. Colour, the black-and-red poultry pattern in the male, with red upperparts and black underparts. Females, brown.

Uses

Dual-purpose. Moderately good performance as both layer and table breed. Said to be very hardy and a good forager.

Houdan —————————

A light breed, developed in France in the early nineteenth century and introduced to Britain in about 1850. Has been subsequently used in the development of other breeds.

Description

The Houdan is a light breed adorned with a feathery topknot and ruff. Mop-headed, it has a bifurcated comb, like butterfly wings. The colour is metallic green-black, mottled and

margined with white. Legs, pinkish white with dark grey mottlings; lobes, white; eyes, red. Tail, long and flowing in male. Weights — male, 7 pounds; female, 6 pounds.

Uses

Dual-purpose, for though a light breed it is heavier than some and produces plump table birds. Good layer. However, it is kept mostly as a show breed.

Indian Game

The alternative name of Cornish Game is more accurate, for the breed originated in Cornwall in the early nineteenth century. Its ancestry is said to have been Old English and Malay Game, with some contribution by the Red Aseel.

Description

The Indian Game has been aptly described as the bulldog of the poultry world. It has a similar massive appearance, very broad chest, legs wide apart and aggressive stance. Very compact and solid. Small pea-type comb. Legs, thick and yellow. Eyes, yellow through orange to red. Colour, black shot with metallic green; some chestnut in the wing. In the female the basic colour of deep chestnut, with lacings of green-black.

Jubilee Game is a colour variety, developed for Queen Victoria's Diamond Jubilee, in which the black becomes white, with some

chestnut on the wings in the male; in the female the predominant colour is white, some feathers having chestnut edgings.

Weights — male, 8 pounds (sometimes more); female, 6 pounds.

Uses

Exclusively a table breed. Sometimes used for crossing with medium breeds to produce good table progeny.

Italiener

A popular European version of the Leghorn.

Description

Whereas in some quarters Leghorn breeders have tended to exaggerate certain characteristics, such as size and shape of comb, refinement of limbs and conformation, etc., the Italiener adheres to the old type of Leghorn. There is a wide range of colours, including white, black, brown, buff, barred and a number of multi-colour patterns. Weights — male, 6 to 8 pounds; female, 5 to 6 pounds.

Uses

Dual-purpose, with the emphasis on egg-laying.

Ixworth

The breed takes its name from Ixworth, Suffolk, where it was developed in the 1930s. Based on Indian Game, Old English Game and Light Sussex.

Description

A heavy breed, of Game type. Broad breast, straddling stance, pea-type comb. Colour, including legs and beak, white. Weights — male, 9 pounds; female, 7 pounds.

Uses A table breed.

Java

An Asiatic breed which came to Britain in the late nineteenth century via America, where it had been much improved. Has been used extensively in the evolution of a number of modern breeds.

Description

A type of jungle fowl. Usually black, though some other colour varieties are, or were, known. Black legs. Comb, single but thick and with very few serrations. Large.

Uses Mainly table.

Jersey Blue

A breed developed in America in the early years of the present century.

Description

Of Plymouth Rock type, the Jersey Blue has slate-coloured plumage, each feather being edged or laced with black. Both sexes have black heads, necks and hackles, and the males have black wing-coverts and a black bar on the wing. Comb, single, erect, serrated and rather large, though slightly drooping in the female. Legs, dark slate. White skin.

Uses

Dual-purpose but a good table bird.

Jersey Giant

Derives its name from the State of New Jersey, U.S.A., where it originated in the late nineteenth century. Ancestry mainly Brahma, Langshan and Black Java.

Description

'Giant' is an accurate adjective. The Jersey

Giant is one of the largest and heaviest breeds. Stocky and massive, with almost horizontal back and broad, deep breast. Two colours, black and white, of which white is the rarer. Black has a greenish sheen. Legs in black variety, also black; beak black with yellow tip; lobes, red; eyes, brown. In white variety, legs and beak whitish; eyes, dark brown or black. Comb, single, serrated and, in male, rather large. Weights — male, 13 pounds; female, 10 pounds.

Uses

Dual-purpose, though primarily a table breed.

Kiwi

A breed developed in New Zealand in the 1920s but never very popular.

Description

The thinking behind the evolution of the breed seems to have been to cross the Silkie with other larger breeds to produce a more economic and larger type while still retaining the Silkie plumage. This was largely achieved. The earliest Kiwis were white, but other colour varieties were later developed.

Uses Dual-purpose.

Kraienkoppe ──────

A breed developed in the mid-1920s in the Netherlands and north Germany.

Description

A game-like breed, with walnut-shaped comb and small wattles. Body long and tail well-rounded. Colour — in male, breast black; upperparts either silver or gold, according to variety; hackles and wing coverts striped; in female, breast salmon-red, body either silver-grey or golden, pencilled with darker hue; hackles striped with black.

Uses

Primarily kept for show purposes, but quite good layers.

La Fleche

A breed of French origin.

Description

Similar to a Black Minorca but rather larger. Colour, black with high green sheen; legs and beak, black; lobes, white. The breed has a curious comb, bifurcated to form two pointed horns, which are large and erect in the male. Weights — male, 8 pounds; female, 7 pounds.

Uses Dual-purpose.

Lakenfelder

A breed of German origin. Very rare.

Description

Leghorn type. Colour, white, apart from glossy black hackles and tail in female; glossy black tail, hackles and speckles on wing coverts in male. Legs, black; lobes, white; comb, erect, single, serrated and rather large. Weights — male, 8 pounds; female, 7 pounds.

Uses Dual-purpose.

Malay

A traditional breed originating in south-east Asia and introduced to Britain in the 1830s. Also now widely spread throughout the world, as a fighting cock.

Description

Typical game-bird conformation and stance, though with much longer legs than Indian Game. Broad-breasted, aggressive appearance. Colours, male black and red; female, buff, with dark brown hackles and central tail-feathers. There are also white, partridge and spangled varieties. Legs and beak, yellow; eyes, yellow or whitish; comb, rose-type and rather broad in front. Weights — male, 11 pounds; female, 9 pounds.

Uses

Apart from its original role as a fighting-cock, it is essentially a table breed.

Malines

A Belgian breed of considerable antiquity, which experienced a period of popularity about the beginning of the present century.

Description

A very large, long-legged breed. The usual colour is barred black and bluish-white, like a Plymouth Rock. Legs and beak, pinkish white; eye, orange; lobes, red. The legs are lightly feathered. Comb, single and erect; but there is a much rarer Turkey-headed variety, which has a pea-type comb and very small wattle. There are also several other colour varieties, including black, blue, white and various combinations of these colours. Weight — male, 11 pounds; female, 9 pounds.

Uses

Primarily a table bird, though it is heavy-boned and carries much weight on its thighs. On the other hand, it puts on weight quickly and the flesh is of excellent quality. Reasonably good performance as an egg producer, but the eggs are rather small. Very hardy and easy to rear.

Manx Rumpie

Little is to be found about this ancient breed in any publication. It is peculiar to the Isle of Man and is now very rare. I first came across it there in the early 1950s, when several flocks of normal-sized birds were in existence. Revisiting the Island about fifteen years later, I at first failed to find any survivors and was assured that no such creatures had ever existed. However, an appeal over the Manx radio prompted a procession of breeders to bring along specimens to the house where I was staying. The breed was evidently surviving in the pens of backyard poultry-keepers, but it had deteriorated dramatically in size. Or, what is more likely, it may have originally existed in two forms, the normal-sized breed and the bantam-sized, of which the former had become extinct since the time of my earlier visit.

Description

The outstanding characteristic of the Manx Rumpie is that, like the Manx cat, it lacks a tail. Not only are there no tail-feathers; there is no bone structure to which they could be anchored. The coccyx is missing. The surviving birds I saw in the Isle of Man in about 1964 were bantam-sized, with rather broad breasts and with legs wide apart, suggesting some game blood in their ancestry. Colours varied, but most were barred, as in the Plymouth Rock.

Uses Dual-purpose.

Marans

The Marans district, from which the breed derives its name, is in western France, near La Rochelle. The Marans became popular in Britain in the middle of the twentieth century and is still kept by poultry-keepers who value the deep, rich brown colour of the eggs. Has been used in the development of other modern breeds.

Description

A neat, compact breed of Sussex type, but rather smaller. The usual colour is barred, with blue-black on white; but there are other colour varieties. Comb, single, serrated and erect but not large. Legs, white; beak, white or horn; eyes, red. Weight — male, 8 pounds; female, 7 pounds.

Uses

Dual-purpose. Consumers are usually willing to pay a little extra for the dark brown eggs, which can compensate for the egg yield being lower than in some of the specialist breeds. The Marans is also a good table bird, maturing quickly and carrying plenty of flesh.

Marsh Daisy

A breed founded in Lancashire in about 1913. Is thought to have descended from a cross between a Malay cock and an Old English Bantam hen, with later admixtures of Old English Game and Sicilian Buttercup.

Description

Compact and rather broad-breasted. Medium size. Cock has brilliant golden upperparts, with black tail and greyish or golden-brown breast; female, brown upperparts, with black edges to hackle feathers, and cream underparts. Comb, rose; legs, greenish; lobes, white; beak, horn; eyes, red.

Uses

Dual-purpose but especially good as a table breed. Moderate as layer but will, if required, give a satisfactory performance for several years. Useful for crossing to produce table progeny.

Modern Game

This is entirely a fanciers' breed, developed from Old English Game, since cock-fighting became illegal.

Description

The Modern Game can be fairly described as the Old English Game with most of its features

exaggerated. The legs and thighs are elongated, till the creature appears to be perched on stilts. The stance has been exaggerated, till the bird is as erect as a penguin. The tail is reduced to a pointed vestige. It takes a fancier to appreciate the beauty of all these new points; to the layman the birds appear grotesque. As with the Old English Game, most combinations of poultry colours are permissible, though each combination has to conform to the stated pattern.

Uses For exhibition.

Modern Langshan

When the Croad Langshan was first introduced it met with some criticism on the grounds that it was identical with the Cochin. To meet that objection some breeders developed characteristics in the breed that would make it unmistakeable, notably the long legs. As a result, two separate breeds evolved, the Croad Langshan, which kept to the original type, and the Modern Langshan.

Description

An upstanding, large breed, with unusually long legs. Colour, black with strong green sheen; legs, black and slightly feathered; lobes, red; beak and eyes, dark brown or black. Legs powerful and set rather far apart. Comb, single, erect and serrated. Weights — male, 10 pounds; female, 8 pounds. There are also rare white and blue varieties.

Uses

A heavy, table breed.

Niederrheiner

A German breed developed as recently as about 1940.

Description

Similar to the Marans in build and general appearance, and one colour variety is very similar to the Marans in colour. Another colour variety, known as the Birchen, has, in

the male, greenish-black underparts and white upperparts with black-margined feathers in hackles and wing-coverts; the female has white head but is otherwise all greenish-black, with black-margined feathers in hackles. Comb, single, erect and serrated. Weights — male, about 7 pounds; female, about 6 pounds.

Uses

Dual-purpose, though inclined towards heaviness. Although the cuckoo variety resembles the Marans it does not produce dark brown eggs.

Norfolk Grey

A breed developed in Norfolk in the 1910s to 1920s, using Game, Leghorn and possibly Australorp parents. Never very plentiful.

Description

Male has white upperparts, with black-edged feathers in hackles and wing-coverts, and green-black underparts; female is all greenish-black, except for black-edged white feathers in hackles, and white head. Legs, dark; eyes, dark; beak, horn. Comb, single, erect, serrated

131

and of medium size. Weight — male, 7 pounds; female, 6 pounds.

Uses

Dual-purpose. Perhaps best as table birds, the cockerels being plump and quick-maturing. Quite good layer, and the eggs are brown and rather large. Hardy.

North Holland Blue

A breed of Dutch origin which has had a period of popularity and has been used extensively in producing modern synthetic breeds but which has now become rather rare.

Description

A barred breed, but rather smaller than the Barred Rock. A plump bird, with long back and well-rounded breast. Comb, medium-sized, erect and single. Legs, feet and beak, white. Legs are lightly feathered. Weights — male, 8 to 10 pounds; female, 7 to 9 pounds.

Uses

Developed primarily as a table breed, though with fairly good egg performance. Has white flesh.

Old English Game

No other breed can claim a greater antiquity. Our present-day birds are in all probability descended from fighting cocks that provided sport in Roman times, and before that similar and doubtless related cocks were bred for fighting in ancient Greece, India and China.

Description

In its long history the breed or type has experienced great diversification. There are, for instance, examples of practically every colour pattern found in poultry. In recent times the breed has tended to split into two main branches. One (the Pit or Oxford type) attempts to retain all the old characteristics of the fighting cock unchanged. The other (the Show or Carlisle type) has been modified to meeting changing show fashions. The traditional English Game birds have broad, powerful breasts, sturdy legs wide apart, erect posture and aggressive stance. The heads are small, with small combs and wattles. Beak, down-curved and powerful; eye, large and prominent. Tail, flowing and flaunting. Spurs, low on the leg and strong. The show type tend to be rather longer in the leg and more shapely in the body. Weights — male, 5 to 6 pounds; female, 4 to 5 pounds. Some of the darker coloured birds have almost black faces, combs and wattles, legs and eyes.

Uses

Now that it can no longer be legally used for fighting, the breed is a fanciers' one, though it can give a useful performance in both egg-laying and table categories. The hens are good mothers.

Old English Pheasant Fowl

Old English Pheasant Fowl

A breed of some antiquity, developed in Yorkshire.

Description

A light breed, probably related to the Hamburgh. Rather small and carries body nearly horizontally. Plump breast. Both sexes have plumage of a rich, golden brown, most feathers being edged with dark brown or black. The luxuriant tail of the cock is greenish black. Comb, rose and tapered. Legs, slate-blue; beak, horn; eyes, red; lobes, white. Weight — male, 6 to 7 pounds; female, 5 to 6 pounds.

Uses

Dual-purpose. Good for both table birds and eggs. Fairly quick-maturing. Hardy and forages well on free range. Has been used quite extensively for crossing with both laying and table breeds.

Orloff ——————————

A breed of Russian origin.

Description

Distinguished by the close feathering, or muffling, around face, which resembles, and is frequently referred to, as beard and whiskers. Moderate size, with fairly broad breast and upright stance. Male is brilliantly coloured, with orange-red wing-coverts, back and hackles, black tail, and underparts deep brown with white edgings to feathers; female, deep red-brown, with black and white margins to many feathers; mufflings in both sexes, grey, brown and black. There are also other colour variations. Legs, yellow; beak, yellow; eyes, red or yellow. Comb, rose-type. Weight — male, 8 pounds; female, 6 pounds.

Uses

Dual-purpose, but mainly a fanciers' breed.

Orpington

Once one of the leading breeds of poultry, the Orpington was originally bred by a Mr William Cook, at Orpington, Kent, and first exhibited at the London Dairy Show in 1886. The foundation breeds were Black Minorca, Black Rock and Croad Langshan. Exported to many other countries, they achieved popularity there, too, especially in Australia, where they were used to produce the Australorp.

Description

A heavy, well-feathered breed, with very deep body and rather short back. Legs, short and black, in the black variety, which is the oldest. The plumage of the black variety is entirely greenish-black, but there are several other colour variations, one of the best-known being the buff, which has handsome, golden-buff plumage. Blue and white Orpingtons were also once quite plentiful. Comb, single, erect, serrated and of medium size. Weight — male, 8 to 10 pounds; female, 6 to 8 pounds.

Uses

Dual-purpose. A splendid table bird and a useful layer. Hardy and adaptable. Much used in producing new breeds.

134

Ostfriesische Mowen

A breed of north German origin which has been exported to several other countries.

Description

Very similar to the Campine. A light, compact breed. Colours — male, white with black tail; female, white covered with lines of small black spangles, but with neck and front white. In the gold variety, the white is replaced by gold in each sex. Comb, single, erect and medium sized in male; in female folded over at end. Weights male, 6 pounds; female,

Uses

Primarily egg-laying, and also a fanciers' breed. Docile and easy to keep.

Phoenix (see YOKOHAMA)

The names Phoenix and Yokohama were formerly interchangeable as terms for the Japanese Long-tailed Fowl. Now it is generally recognised that the Yokohama has a rose comb, the Phoenix a single comb; otherwise they are virtually identical.

Description

There are several colour varieties, and the black and red colour pattern (green-red upperparts, green-black underparts, in the male) seems to be the most frequent.

Plymouth Rock

A breed developed in the mid-nineteenth century in the U.S.A. and Canada; from thence exported to Britain, where it became very popular. Foundation breeds are said to have been the Black Java and Dominique, both American.

Description

A heavy, solid breed. The commonest colour variety is the Barred, in which each feather has bars of blue-white and greenish black. There are also Buff, White, Black and several other colour varieties. Legs, yellow, except in black and blue varieties. Comb, single, erect, serrated and of medium size. Weight — male, 8 to 10 pounds; female, 6 to 8 pounds.

Uses

Dual-purpose. Excellent table bird. Much used in the development of modern auto-sexing breeds.

Poland, or POLISH

Whether this breed originated in Poland, as its name implies, or in some other part of Europe is not known. It is of considerable antiquity, having been described in the early seventeenth century.

Description

Classified as a light breed, of small to medium size. Its most conspicuous characteristic is its crest or topknot, which consists of a mop of feathers, falling down evenly around the head and almost hiding the face. There are many colour varieties. In a number of them the body is of one colour, as black or blue, while the crest is white; in others the crest is of the same colour as the body. In the Gold-laced and Silver-laced each feather is gold or silver marginned with black. These laced varieties have muffling, or beards, around and under the face, as well as crests. Legs are normally slate-blue. Combs are generally invisible and sometimes non-existent. Weight — male, 6 pounds; female, 5 pounds.

Uses

Chiefly a fanciers' breed. Under favourable conditions are fair to good producers of eggs. Moderate as table birds.

Redcap, or DERBYSHIRE REDCAP

The name refers to the shape of the comb, which is of rose type but very large, broad and pointed at the end farthest from the beak. It does indeed look like a red cap. The breed has been well established in Derbyshire, Yorkshire and neighbouring counties for centuries, at least as far back as the fourteenth century.

Description

The comb is the most conspicuous distinguishing feature. The breed is a rather small one, with a broad, plump breast and flat back. The cock has golden-red upperparts, though the feathers of the hackles and wing coverts are margined with black; the underparts, the tail and a bar on the wing are metallic green-black. The female is rich brown, each feather being edged with black. Legs, dark grey; beak, horn; eyes, red. Weight — male, 6 pounds; female, 5 pounds.

Uses

A light breed, though dual-purpose, for it has been kept largely on hill farms with little selection of stock. A good converter of food, it forages actively and is very hardy. Although small it is plump and its meat is of good quality.

Rheinlander

A German breed, developed in the Rhineland in the 1880s.

Description

A neat, light, compact breed of the Hamburgh type. Rounded body and very fine tail. Colours — varied, including white, blue and barred, but with black the most frequent, the black having a metallic greenish sheen. Comb — rose; lobes, small, round and white. Weights — male, 5 to 6 pounds; female, 4 to 5 pounds.

Uses

Primarily layers, noted for their egg production and longevity, but also produces a small but meaty table carcase.

Scots Dumpy

The term 'dumpy' refers to the extreme shortness of the legs, a genetical characteristic akin to dwarfism which is associated with a heavy mortality rate in the embryo chicks. For all that, it is a very old breed. Similar types are known in several European countries and existed at least as early as the seventeenth century.

Scots Grey

Description

A squat and somewhat ungainly breed, which waddles about on its short legs, the shanks of which should be no more than 1½ inches long. Colour, usually barred black and white, as in the Barred Rock. There are also black and grey colour varieties. Combs, either simple or rose. Legs and beak, mottled black and white; eyes, red. Weight — male, 7 pounds; female, 6 pounds.

Uses

Classified as a light breed but in fact dual-purpose. Now kept mostly as a novelty but very rare.

Scots Grey

A Scottish breed, known in the eighteenth century.

Description

Not unlike a Barred Rock but of lighter build. It has long legs and erect stance; rounded breast; rather long tail. Colour, barred, each feather having black bars on a bluish-white ground. Legs, white or mottled; beak, white; eyes, yellow. Comb, single, serrated and erect. Weight — male, 7 pounds; female, 5 pounds.

Uses

Dual-purpose, though classified as light. Quite good as both layers and table birds. Hardy, but fattens quickly on a generous diet.

Shamo

A Japanese game breed, very like the Malay.

Description

Typical game appearance, with wide but straight back, broad breast, legs astraddle, long, curved neck, broad head and strong, curved beak. Legs, stout but shorter than in Malay. Colour — black and red pattern. Weights — male, about 11 pounds; female, 9 pounds.

Uses

For show purposes and table.

Sherwood

A breed developed in America in the early years of the present century but never particularly popular.

Description

Briefly, a white edition of the Plymouth Rock, but with feathered legs.

Uses Dual-purpose.

Sicilian Buttercup

Apparently this breed originated in Sicily, where it had existed for centuries. In the second half of the nineteenth century some were taken to the U.S.A., from whence it was introduced to Britain about 1912.

Description

One of the most distinctive features of this breed is the remarkable comb, which is bowl-shaped and serrated, with the end 'tooth' enlarged and elongated. The whole resembles two separate single and serrated combs joined at each end, with a concave area between. Colour — male, a golden or orange red, lightest

and brightest on the hackles, darker and duller on the under parts; tail and wing coverts green-black. Female, light golden brown, flecked and spangled with black. There are also other colour varieties, including white, brown and silver. Legs, greenish; lobes, white and red; beak, yellow and black; eyes, red. Weights — male, 6 to 7 pounds; females, 5 to 6 pounds.

Uses

Dual-purpose. Hardy and adaptable in their native country, but elsewhere generally regarded as a fanciers' breed.

Sicilian Flowerbird

When, after the first world war, Sicilian Buttercups, from stock imported from the U.S.A., became quite popular as a show breed in Britain, several breeders went back to the original home of the breed, Sicily, and made direct imports. Attempts were then made to have these new introductions recognised as a distinct breed, but success was modest and ephemeral, and the breed faded into oblivion, though it should be possible to recreate it.

Description

It closely resembles the Sicilian Buttercup, as was only natural, but was much smaller, the weight of the male being about 4 pounds, that of the female only about 3 pounds.

Silkie

Almost certainly this breed originated in east Asia — some think in Japan, others in China or south-east Asia — but a long time ago, for it has been known and bred in Britain for very many years.

Description

A bird of remarkable appearance. The feathers are reduced to almost hair-like dimensions, giving the birds the appearance of being clad in fluffy fur, something like an Angora rabbit. In addition, both the flesh and the skin are of a deep violet hue, becoming more purple on the exposed face and wattles. Although classified as large poultry, Silkies are about midway between normal poultry and bantams in size. They are heavily plumaged, giving them a 'powder-puff' appearance, with a fluffy crest or topknot. The birds hold themselves erect but have a short, horizontal back, and their legs are so short that the plumage of the breast and stomach often touches the ground. Legs and toes are lightly feathered. Comb, broad, almost round, with small protuberances. Legs, grey; eyes, black; lobes, usually green-blue but sometimes purple; beak, slate-blue.

Weights — male, 3 pounds; female, 2 pounds. There are several colour varieties, of which buff, blue and white are the commonest.

Uses

An all-purpose breed, though the colour of the flesh is against it as a table bird. Laying performance is quite good, the eggs being large compared with the size of the bird. The chicks are hardy and easily reared, though there is often a fairly high proportion of broken eggs during incubation, due to brittle shells. Broodiness is a characteristic of the Silkie, and the hens are therefore often employed for hatching bantam eggs.

Spanish

One of the older breeds of the western Mediterranean and among the ancestors of the Minorca.

Description

A long-legged and rather ungainly bird. The most distinctive feature is the white face and very long and large white lobes, which meet in front of the neck. Legs are set well apart. Comb, single, erect and serrated in the cock, falling to one side in the hen. Colour, black with green sheen. Legs, purplish-grey; beak, horn; eyes, black. Weights — male, 7 pounds; female, 6 pounds.

Uses

Primarily a laying breed, producing good quantities of large eggs. Hardy and adaptable.

Sultan

A breed which apparently originated in the Near East and was introduced to Britain from Turkey in 1854. Never plentiful.

Description

Very similar in appearance to the Poland, having the same crest and muffling which almost conceal the face and eyes. The plumage is dense, and the legs and feet are heavily feathered. The body is broad and deep, the back straight and short; legs are short. Colour, white. Comb, small and bifurcated, almost hidden by crest. Legs, bluish; beak, white or blue; eyes, red. Weights — male, 6 pounds; female, 4 to 5 pounds.

Uses

Mainly a fanciers' breed but are good layers, their white eggs being large in proportion to the size of the bird. Thrifty and active. Economical to keep.

Sumatra Game

Sultan

Sumatra Game

A breed originating in Sumatra, where it was, and perhaps is, bred largely for producing fighting cocks.

Description

A long-bodied, long-necked breed of considerable elegance. The head is small and surmounted by a small, pea-type comb. The long tail is carried droopingly, more like a pheasant than ordinary domestic poultry. Colour, black with metallic green sheen. Legs, black or olive; eyes, dark red or black. Comb, face, lobes and wattles are either black or very dark red, the lobes and wattles being very small. Weights — male, 6 pounds; female, 4 to 5 pounds.

Uses

Apart from its employment as a fighting breed in its native land, the Sumatra Game is, in western countries, a fanciers' breed. They are fairly good layers, of white eggs, and, being broad-breasted, are useful table birds.

141

Surrey

The term 'Surrey' was more properly applied to a process for producing a white-fleshed, well-fattened table bird but came in time to refer to the type of bird best suited to the trade. Based on Light Sussex, Indian Game and White Wyandotte, with possibly some other blood, the breed was standardised in 1938.

Description

A plump, heavy breed. Colour, white, with white beaks and legs. Comb, rose and of medium size. Weights — male, 9 to 10 pounds; female, 7 to 8 pounds.

Uses

Excellent table bird.

Transylvanian Naked Neck

A breed originating in Transylvania. When first brought to Britain it was popularly thought to be a cross between a fowl and a turkey, which, of course, was a completely erroneous idea.

Description

An ugly bird, which looks as though it has lost all its head and neck feathers through feather-pecking or moulting, thus acquiring a vulturine appearance. A fairly large breed. Colours, usually green-black, but there are also white, red and barred varieties. Comb, single, erect, serrated and rather small. A line of feathers along the top of the head tends to look like a heavily-pencilled eyebrow. Legs and beak, slate-grey; eyes, red.

Uses

A novelty breed, but dual-purpose and quite hardy.

Voldarno

A breed developed in Italy.

Description

Light birds, similar to the Leghorn but lighter. Colour — two varieties; white, with yellow legs; black, with grey legs. Comb, single, erect and serrated in cock; dropping in hen. Weights, male, 4 to 6 pounds; female, 3 to 5 pounds.

Uses

Excellent layer. Hardy and thrifty.

Vorwerk

A breed first developed in north Germany in about 1912.

Description

A breed of Leghorn type, very similar to the Lakenfelder but buff in colour, with glossy black hackles, tail and speckles on wing coverts. Comb, rather large, single and serrated. Weights — male, 8 to 9 pounds; female, 7 to 8 pounds.

Uses

Dual-purpose.

Vorwerk

Welsummer

A breed of Dutch origin, introduced to Britain in 1928 and achieving for a time considerable popularity. The name is derived from the village of Welsum, where the breed was developed. Ancestry is thought to include the Barnevelder and Brown Leghorn, with perhaps the Wyandotte.

Description

A handsome black-and-red breed. In male, the upperparts are golden red, with green-black tail and wing-bar; the underparts are green-black, with red flecks on breast. Female is red-brown, distinctly darker on back than on breast; hackles, brown with gold edgings. Legs and beak, yellow; eyes, orange. Comb, single, erect, serrated and of medium size. A compact, well-shaped breed, with fairly deep body and broad breast. Weight — male, 7 pounds; female, 6 pounds.

Uses

Classified as a light breed and developed mainly for egg production, though it is a useful dual-purpose bird. Lays a large, brown egg.

Welsummer

Yokohama

This is the name generally given in Britain to the Japanese Long-tailed fowl, bred for centuries in Japan both as a fighting cock and for exhibition. In extreme instances in Japan the tail has been known to reach lengths of 18 to 20 feet. The *Phoenix* is sometimes considered a distinct variety from the Yokohama, but the only difference is that whereas the Yokohama has a rose comb the Phoenix's comb is single.

Description

A sleek, alert bird, holding its tail low, like a pheasant, though its head erect. Light but broad-breasted, neat and compact, and with obvious Game affinities. There are several colour varieties, the most frequent in the Yokohama being the Red Saddled, in which (in the male) the upperparts are white with the exception of a deep red bar across the wings and back; the underparts are pink, with feathers margined with white. In the female, the coloration is the same, except that the saddle is of the same colour as the breast. Legs and beak, yellow; eyes, red. Weights — male, 4 to 6 pounds; female, 2½ to 4 pounds.

Wyndham Black

An auto-sexing breed. The chicks are hatched black, the males having white throats and fronts, while the females are either all black or have a greyish shading on the neck. Probably extinct.

Description

A long-legged, long-necked breed with erect carriage. Colour, entirely greenish-black. Legs, black; beak, dark horn; eyes, yellow. Comb, single, erect, of medium size and deeply serrated; in females the comb falls to one side. Weights — male, 7 pounds; female, 5 pounds.

Uses

Dual-purpose.

Yokohama

Uses

A fanciers' breed, but quite useful table birds, though small. Also good layers, though the eggs are only about bantam size. Excellent hens for incubating. Thrifty, economical, hardy and quick-maturing.

York

A synthetic breed developed between the wars in Yorkshire, without attracting much attention. Probably extinct.

Description

A bird of Sussex type, with conventional red-and-black coloration (red upperparts, black underparts and tail) in the male, partridge or buff-brown in the female, but smaller than the Sussex. Comb, single, erect and serrated. Legs, white.

Uses

Dual-purpose, though with an emphasis on table qualities. Matures quickly. Lays brown eggs.

Geese, Ducks and Turkeys

Geese and ducks are common and widely distributed throughout the northern hemisphere, and the young of most species are easily domesticated if taken at the nestling state.

Old World geese are derived mainly from the Grey Lag Goose (*Anser anser*), though the Chinese Goose has a separate origin in the wild *Cygnopsis cygnoides*. Geese were domesticated from early times in ancient Egypt, Babylonia, Greece and elsewhere. There has, however, been no great multiplication of breeds, for the reason that domestic geese mate readily with wild ones and so tend to maintain more or less the original type.

Much the same applies to the domestic duck, which is derived mainly from the Mallard (*Anas platyrhyncha*). Wild Mallard quite frequently associate and mate with domestic ducks, and some of the older breeds, such as the Rouen, display typical Mallard colours.

Turkeys were first introduced to Europe in 1523 or 1524 from Mexico, where they were already domesticated. Within less than fifty years they were being bred extensively and commercially. White varieties were apparently developed before their introduction to Europe.

TOP OF PAGE **Saxony ducks and Brecon Buff goslings**

Geese

Brecon Buff

Based on the traditional buff-coloured geese of central Wales, the Brecon Buff was established as a breed in 1934.

Description

Of medium size, compact and full-breasted, the Brecon Buff caters for the demand for a plump but rather small goose. Colour — a golden buff, with lighter edgings to the feathers. Legs, orange. Weights — male, 13 to 14 pounds; female, 11 to 12 pounds.

Uses

A neat, well-fleshed table goose; also a good layer. Very hardy.

Roman

A breed, thought to be of Italian origin, which has spread quite extensively in western Europe, though its present numbers and status are unknown.

Description

A neat, compact little goose, about half the size of the massive Embden-Toulouse. Colour, pure white; legs, feet and bill, orange. Weights — male, 12 to 13 pounds; female, 10 to 11 pounds.

Uses

Dual-purpose. Matures quickly, the goslings being capable of reaching a weight of 8 pounds within about four months. Very hardy and quite a good layer.

Pilgrim

An old English breed, known in the early seventeenth century.

Description

A goose of medium size. This is one of those breeds in which there is a colour difference between the sexes. The whites are ganders, the greys geese.

Uses

Dual-purpose.

Sebastopol

A breed of Russian origin.

Description

The most distinctive feature of this breed is the long, curled feathers which form a kind of mantle reaching nearly to the ground. In this respect they resemble the Frizzled breed of poultry. Legs, feet and bill are orange; the plumage entirely white. Weights — male, 10 pounds; female, 9 pounds.

Uses

Quite a good table bird but usually kept for ornamental purposes.

Ducks

Abacot Ranger

A breed of obscure origins and status. It is said to have originated from crosses between White Indians Runners and Khaki-Campbells, with perhaps some Aylesbury blood as well. May now be extinct as a pure breed.

Description

A medium-sized duck. Colour, mainly white but with fawn upperparts, the drakes having a brown head and neck.

Uses

In the 1920s the breed was producing good laying performance.

Baldwin

Description

A handsome duck, not unlike the Rouen. In build and carriage it is about midway between the Aylesbury and the Runners. The coloration is the handsome mixture familiar in mallards. The head and neck are iridiscent green, the underparts rose-colour. Between the breast and the neck is a broad band of white. The upperparts are deep blue, with some pencilling on the flanks. In the wings is a vivid blue bar, margined by white and black. Legs and feet, orange; beak, yellowish green. Eyes, dark brown. The female, as is normal in ducks, is much more modestly dressed, mostly in fawn but with a creamy-white breast. Weights — male, 10 pounds; female, 8 to 9 pounds.

Uses

Dual-purpose.

Bali

Introduced to Britain from the East Indian island of Bali in 1925.

Description

The most noticeable feature of this duck is its crest, an almost globular topknot of feathers set on the exact centre of the head. Both male and females have this crest, though in the females it tends to droop to one side. The body is streamlined, like that of the Indian Runner, though the Bali is larger and heavier. Colour — pure white, with beak, legs and feet orange-yellow. Eye, blue. This bird has the upright stance of the Indian Runner and should hold its body at an angle of 60° to 80° to the horizontal. Weights — male, 5 pounds, female, 4 pounds.

Uses

Primarily a laying breed.

Black East Indian

The breed is said to have originated in India, but has long been acclimatized in other countries, notably the U.S.A. and Canada. Darwin knew it as the Labrador Duck.

Description

This is a diminutive duck, a bantam among ducks. It is very small but beautifully compact and with a well-rounded figure. Its colour is entirely a glossy green-black; the legs and bill are dark to match. Weights — male, 2 pounds; female, about 1½ pounds.

Uses

The Black East Indian is too small to have much commercial value (though its flesh is delicious) and is generally kept as an ornamental feature on private waters. It can fly very well and so should be pinioned unless kept in a pen roofed with wire-netting. The female can be safely allowed to hatch her own eggs.

149

Cayuga

It takes its name from Lake Cayuga, in New York State, where it was introduced about the middle of the nineteenth century, but is supposed to have been developed in South America, from the East Indian breed.

Description

Almost identical with the Black East Indian, except in size, it being very much larger. The plumage is the same metallic green-black, but the legs and feet are orange-brown. Weights — male, 8 pounds; female, 7 pounds.

Uses

Primarily a table breed. Unlike many breeds of ducks, the Cayuga will hatch her own ducklings quite satisfactorily and is a good mother. Egg-laying ability — no more than moderate.

Crested

A very old breed, originating on the European continent and possibly in Holland, though no records are available.

Description

The most noticeable feature of the breed is the crest, which is globular, though not too large. It looks amusingly like the mob cap that Mother Goose wears in Christmas pantomimes. A large, heavy duck, rather similar to the Aylesbury. The general colour is white, though other colours are permissible. Feet, legs and beak (in the white variety), bright orange-yellow. Weights — male, 7 pounds, female, 6 pounds. The crest, incidentally, is not apparently a dominant characteristic, for quite a large proportion of ducklings hatched from pure-bred stock lack it.

Uses

A good dual-purpose breed. Lays quite well and also produces good carcases. The young mature rapidly.

Gimbsheimer

A west German breed of recent origin.

Description

A long-bodied, heavy breed with short legs, like the Orpington. Colour, blue-grey throughout. Weights — male, 5 to 7½ pounds; female, a little lighter.

Uses

Dual-purpose.

Crested ducks

Magpie

A breed developed in Wales in the early years of the twentieth century. It must not be confused by the larger, heavier but somewhat similar Muscovy duck (which, besides being much more plentiful, is technically a goose).

Description

A large duck, with deep and broad breast and a very long body. There are two main varieties, the Black and the Blue. In both of them the predominant colour is white. In the black, the top of the head and the whole of the back and wing coverts are black; in the blue, these areas are blue. The legs, feet and beak are orange-yellow. Weights — male, 6 to 7 pounds; female, 5 to 6 pounds. The blue is the rarer of the two varieties.

Uses

Dual-purpose. Performs reasonably well as both a layer and a table bird but breaks no records.

Orpington

This breed was developed at his home in Orpington, Kent, by Mr William Cook, who also established the Orpington breed of fowls. It is thought to have Aylesbury, Rouen, Cayuga and Indian Runner blood in its make-up.

Description

A heavy breed, with a long, sleek body and short legs. Colour — a golden buff, with the face, head and neck several shades darker in the male. There are also a few other rare colour varieties, notably the blue. Legs, beak and feet — orange-red. Weights — male, 5 to 7½ pounds; female, much the same, though perhaps ½-pound lighter.

Uses

Dual-purpose. An excellent layer and a good producer of table carcases. Ducklings mature quickly.

Pekin

An oriental breed introduced to Britain and western Europe in the 1870s. It came to the U.S.A. at about the same time, and from thence many were shipped to Europe. Though popular in both Europe and America, the Pekin lost favour in Britain through the insistence of breeders on maintaining the original colour, yellow.

Description

The original yellow has now been modified to 'creamy-white'. Legs, feet and beak are bright orange. The Pekin combines the peculiar upright carriage of the Runner with the massive body of the Aylesbury, being particularly heavy about the stern. Weights — males, 9 pounds; females, 8 pounds.

Uses

Dual-purpose. In the States it is kept primarily as a table bird, in which role it excels. On the other hand, it is often used for crossing with the Aylesbury to produce progeny with a better egg-laying capacity. Its annual egg-yield is quoted as up to 130.

Penguin

A traditional breed established perhaps for centuries in Cumberland. Present status unknown.

Description

A rather small black duck with a few white markings. Of Indian Runner type. Weights — male, about 6 pounds; female, about 5 pounds.

Uses

Dual-purpose. A good table bird and fairly good layer. Very hardy in its own environment.

Rouen

The Rouen seems to be the domesticated edition of the Mallard, or common Wild Duck, improved by centuries of breeding in northern France.

Description

A massive, heavy-bodied breed, the Rouen displays exactly the Mallard colours — glossy green head, purple-bronze breast, rump and back greenish black, underparts grey with light and dark vermiculations. The female is brown, with pencilled markings. Legs and feet, orange red; beak, green or yellow. Weights — male, 10 pounds; female, 9 pounds.

Uses

Essentially a table duck, its great size being matched by flesh of excellent flavour. As an egg-layer it is poor. Fertility is also low, and a breeding pen should allow not more than three ducks to every drake. The ducklings, though of impressive size when finished, are rather slow to mature. The chief role of the Rouen in modern breeding, therefore, is for crossing with other breeds to iron out these defects and yet retain the splendid table qualities of the Rouen.

Saxony

A German breed, standardised in 1957, with much Rouen and Pekin blood in its make-up.

Description

Very similar to the Silver Appleyard in both conformation and colour. Female, rather bluer than the Silver Appleyard, with dark stripe over eye.

Uses

Dual-purpose.

Silver Appleyard

Description

Similar to the Mallard in size and build but much lighter in colour. The males have silver-grey backs, iridescent green heads, reddish-brown breasts and a white demarcation band between the green and the brown. The female's plumage is almost entirely silvery brown.

Uses Dual-purpose.

Stanbridge White

This breed was developed in the early decades of the present century at Romsey, Hampshire, using only pure white sports of the Magpie breed.

Description

A snow-white edition of the Magpie Duck, the Stanbridge White is virtually identical with that breed except in colour, which, however, is stable in the newer breed.

Uses

Selection for white coloration also produced a breed with a much better egg-laying capacity, while still retaining its performance as a table bird. Very hardy.

154

Swedish

The breed is said to have originated in Sweden but has no recorded history. Has at times been quite popular in America.

Description

A large, heavy breed, very similar to the Rouen but with different coloration, which is a slaty-blue, unrelieved by any other colour except for a white splotch on the throat. Weights — male, 10 pounds; female, 9 pounds.

Uses

A massive, well-fleshed table bird.

Welsh Harlequin

This breed was developed as recently as 1949 from the Khaki-Campbell.

Description

Closely resembles the Khaki-Campbell in build; while in appearance it is very similar to the Mallard. The colours in the drake are Mallard colours, with the difference that the back is mottled cream and brown. As in the Rouen, there is a conspicuous white collar. The female shows much more cream coloration, on the breast and abdomen and, with a mottled effect, on the back. Head and neck are fawn. Weights — male, 5½ to 6 pounds; female, 4½ to 5 pounds.

Uses

Bred to be an egg-producer, the breed is said to have an improved performance over the parent Khaki-Campbell. Is exceptionally docile.

Turkeys

Bourbon Red

An American breed distinguished by its dark brownish-red colour, relieved by white wing and tail feathers.

Buff

A breed developed in America. Colours can be various shades of buff or fawn, with white wing and tail feathers.

Cambridge Bronze

An early breed probably developed by crossing the black turkeys, which were the first to be imported to Britain, with the Mexican Bronze, which came a little later. Having contributed to a number of improved breeds which superseded it, it is now probably extinct.

A bird of medium size, but well-fleshed.

Narragansett ———

A breed developed at a fairly early date in Rhode Island, U.S.A., by crossing Cambridge and Black turkeys. The colours are glossy black, with each feather margined with light grey.

Norfolk Black ———

This is probably the oldest of British breeds of turkey, deriving directly from the black turkeys first brought to England in the 1520s.

Description

Colour — a glossy, purple-black throughout; legs, feet and bill also black. Rather smaller and shorter in the legs than the bronze varieties.

Uses

Table bird.

Slate, or BLUE

A breed of American origin. Colour — entirely slate-blue throughout, including legs, feet and beak.

Epilogue ———

This is a continuing story. So far we have arrived at the end of only the first chapters. Concern for the survival of rare breeds of livestock began to be widely expressed only in the 1960s, although early in the 1950s I was noting with regret, in articles in *The Field*, the decline of such breeds of cattle as the Old Gloucestershire (an excellent herd survived in Colesbourne Park, the home of the late Colonel Elwes) and the British White and of the Wiltshire Horn, Cotswold and other breeds of sheep. In the late 1950s I attempted, prematurely as it happens, to find a sufficient number of breeders interested in forming a society for the Jacob sheep.

For a time Whipsnade Zoo served as a repository of specimens of rare breeds for which no other home could be found. Under pressure of space it passed on to the University of Reading its stock of certain breeds. Around 1968 the University regretfully decided that it could no longer maintain them and certain other rare specimens it had acquired from other sources, with the result that a stock of some of the surviving Soay, Cotswold and the very rare Portland sheep were looking for a home.

At this juncture the Royal Agriculture Society of England, well established on its permanent site at Stoneleigh, Warwickshire, now the National Agricultural Centre, stepped in. It set up a working party to survey the situation and initiate a programme for saving rare breeds, which led to the formation of the Rare Breeds Survival Trust in 1973. Nucleus stock of a number of rare breeds was deposited at Stoneleigh, where they still flourish, while other collections began quickly to be built up by private enterprise, an outstanding venture being the Cotswold Farm Park at Guiting Power, Gloucestershire, belonging to Mr. J. Henson, now Chairman of the Trust. A monthly magazine, *The Ark*, was founded in 1974 and has done much to foster the remarkable interest in rare breeds that has been aroused. Members have flocked to join not only the Trust but the individual breed societies, of which many new ones have been formed.

In the same year as the formation of the R.A.S.E.'s working party a Biosphere Conference in Paris also recommended that steps should be taken to preserve the heritage of genetic variety that seemed in danger of being drastically diminished by concentration on what appeared at the moment to be the most productive lines. In 1972 the Stockholm Conference on the Environment proposed the compilation of a catalogue of rare breeds. In 1975 the FAO took a step towards this end by publishing *A Pilot Study on the Conservation of Animal Genetic Resources*. 1978 saw the publication of a survey of progress to date, *The Chance to Survive*, by Lawrence Alderson, Technical Adviser to the Rare Breeds Survival Trust.

Meantime, parallel movements to the British have been started in France, the Netherlands and the United States of America, and others will doubtless follow.

The scope is virtually limitless. Our survey has covered most of the rare breeds of Britain and what appear to be the most important of the rare breeds of Europe but it cannot be exhaustive. A French investigation in 1974 revealed no fewer than 22 rare breeds of cattle, 36 of sheep, 9 of pigs, 4 of goats and 4 of horses. Similar surveys in other countries would probably be equally productive, especially in those where no official centrally controlled breeding policy has been operating and where, therefore, pockets of the old breeds have been permitted to survive.

The situation has been by no means completely explored in Britain. Readers may note my experiences in search of the Old Manx breed of 'Rumpie' poultry. Similar discoveries may still be made, though probably most of the work has already been done with the larger livestock.

There is also considerable scope for enthusiasts with an acre or two to help in preserving rare breeds. Not much space is required for pens of poultry, and it is just as easy to keep a rare breed as a well-established one. With sheep specimens of a number of rare breeds may be run together; they need to be kept separate only in the mating season. With ponies and horses, more funds are needed to outbid horsemeat dealers at fairs and dispersal sales.

The following addresses will be found useful.

Australia

Royal Agricultural Society of N.S.W.
Showground, Driver Avenue, Paddington,
N.S.W. 2021

Royal Agricultural Society of Victoria
Epsom Road, Ascot Vale, Victoria 3032

Royal National Agricultural Assoc. of Queensland
Exhibition Grounds, Gregory Terrace, Fortitude
Valley, Qld 4006

Royal Agricultural Society of South Australia Inc.
Royal Showground, Wayville, S.A. 5034

Royal Agricultural Society of Western Australia (Inc)
The Rothmans Building, Royal Showgrounds,
Claremont, W.A. 6010

Royal Agricultural Society of Tasmania
The Rothmans Building, Royal Showgrounds,
Glenorchy, Tas. 7010

CATTLE

Australian Registered Cattle Breeders' Association
P.O. Box 131, North Sydney, N.S.W. 2060

Chianina Society of Australia
Incorporating Marchigiana, Romagnola,
17th Level, Capital Centre, Hilton Hotel, Pitt Street,
Sydney, N.S.W. 2000

Dairy Shorthorn Association of Australia
Royal Showgrounds, Epsom Road, Ascot Vale,
Vic. 3032

Registered Dairy Cattle Association of Australia
Box 4317, G.P.O., Sydney, N.S.W. 2001

SHEEP

New South Wales Sheepbreeders' Association
Box 4317, G.P.O., Sydney 2001

Australian Society of Breeders of British Sheep
Royal Showgrounds, Epsom Road, Ascot Vale,
Vic. 3032

Black and Coloured Sheep Breeders' Association of
Australia
c/o P. Hodann, P.O. Box 17, Mittagong, N.S.W. 2575

Association of Stud Sheep Breeders of Australia
W. J. Martin, Balmoral Balmorn, Sandt Creek,
S.A. 5350

PIGS

Australian Pig Breeders' Society
33 Bong Bong Street, Kiama, N.S.W. 2533

B. L. Whip
183 North Quay, Brisbane, Qld 4000

W. G. Swanson
Box 189 PO, Kiama, N.S.W. 2533

H. J. Clappison
Royal Showgrounds, Epsom Road, Ascot Vale,
Vic 3032

R. H. Sedsman
Showgrounds, Wayville, S.A. 5034

J. F. Howson
Box 135 PO, Claremont, W.A. 6010

D. L. Paterson
National Showgrounds, 20 College Street, Launceston,
Tas. 7250

POULTRY

Poultry Research Advisory Committee
c/o Department of Primary Industry, Edmund Barton
Building, Barton, A.C.T. 2600

Belgium

POULTRY

Fédération Nationale des Sociétés d'Aviculteurs
Familiaux et d'Eleveurs de Lapins
rue Estroit 6, 5640 — Mettet

Canada

CATTLE

Canadian Cattle Breeders' Association
P.O. Box 547, Granby, Quebec, Canada

Canadian Highland Cattle Association
R.R.6, Shelburne, Ontario

Canadian Pinzgauer Association
202-528 - 9th Avenue S.W., Calgary, Alberta

Canadian Red Poll Association
P.O. Box 15, Francis, Saskatchewan

Canadian Romagnola Association
Site 2, P.O. Box 2, R.R. 3, High River, Alberta

Canadian Tarentaise Association
P.O. Box 1270, Fort Macleod, Alberta

Salers Association of Canada
Suite 201, 1200 - 26th Avenue S.E., Calgary, Alberta

SHEEP

Sheep Association
Ministry of Agriculture & Food,
Newmarket Plaza, Newmarket, Ontario L3Y 2N1

PIGS

Canadian Swine Breeders Association
R.R. No. 5, Cambridge (Galt), Ontario N1R 5S6

POULTRY

Canadian Poultry Council
5233 Dundas Street W., Islington, Ontario M9B 1A6

Finland

The Finnish Animal Breeding Association
P.O. Box 40, SF — 01301 Vantaa 30

France

Association pour la Diffusion à l'étranger des Techniques
de l'Élevage Français 43-45 rue de Naples, 75008 Paris

CATTLE

Herd Book Salers
26 rue du 139e   Regiment-d'infanterie, 15006
Aurillac

UPRA Tarentaise
11 rue Metropole, 73000 Chambéry

POULTRY

Société Centrale d'Aviculture de France
34 rue de Lille, 75007 Paris

Germany

Auswertungs-und Informationsdienst für Ernährung,
Landwirtschaft und Forsten e.V.
AID, Postfach 20 0708, 5300 Bonn 2

Arbeitsgemeinschaft Deutscher Tierzüchter e.V.
Adenauerallee 174, 5300 Bonn

Ireland

Rare Breeds Survival Trust
D. G. Couper,
Cornahir House, Tyrrellspass, Co. Westmeath

CATTLE

The Kerry Cattle Society of Ireland
Cahirnane, Killarney, Co. Kerry

The Irish Agricultural Museum
Johnstown Castle, Wexford

The Agricultural Institute
Dunsinea, Castleknock, Co. Dublin

PIGS

The Agricultural Institute
Moorepare Research Centre, Fermoy, Co. Cork

SHEEP

The Agricultural Institute
Belclare, Tuam, Co. Galway

Netherlands

Mrs. A. T. Clason,
Stichting Zaldzame Huisdieren, Poststraat 6, 9712
E R Groningen

CATTLE

Vereniging 'Het Friesch Rundvee Stamboek' (F.R.S.)
Zuiderplein 4, P.O.B. 202, Leeuwarden. Tel:5100-
29341

Koninklijke Vereniging het Nederlandsche Rundvee-
Stamboek (N.R.S.)
Stadhoudersplantsoen 24, The Hague. Tel: 70-394965

Ver. 'Het Nederlands Aalstrepen- of Witrikkenstam-
boek' (rare breeds)
Govert Flinckstraat 16, Papendrecht. Tel. 78-55486

SHEEP

Centraal Bureau voor de Schapenfokkerij in
Nederland (C.B.S.)
Landbouwhuis, Alkmaar. Tel: 72-122020

PIGS

Centraal Bureau voor de Varkensfokkerij in
Nederland
Oranjesingel 74, Nijmegen. Tel: 80-226355

POULTRY

Koninklijke Nederlandse Vereniging 'Ornithophilia'
Koekoekstraat 31, Leerdam. Tel: 3451-3820

New Zealand

Ministry of Agriculture and Fisheries
Box 2298, Wellington

CATTLE

New Zealand Dairy Breeders' Federation
Tel: 78-641

Galloway Cattle Society of New Zealand
Box 49, Clevedon

New Zealand Red Poll Cattle Breeders' Association
(Inc)
Irwell, RD3, Christchurch

SHEEP

New Zealand Sheep Breeders' Association
Box 9002, Christchurch

Southdown Sheep Society of New Zealand
Box 636, Blenheim

PIGS

New Zealand Pig Breeders' Association
Box 85, Palmerston North

POULTRY

New Zealand Poultry Board
Second Floor, Poultry Board Building, 65 Victoria
Street, Wellington, Box 379

Switzerland

CATTLE

Commission of Swiss Cattle Breeders Federations
Villettemattstrasse 9, Postfach, CH-3000, Bern 14

United Kingdom

Rare Breeds Survival Trust
Market Place, Haltwhistle, Northumberland

CATTLE

National Cattle Breeders' Association
Cholesbury, Nr. Tring, Herts.

Belted Galloway Cattle Society
49 Tylers Acre Avenue, Edinburgh EH12 7JE

Chillingham Wild Cattle Association
Estate Office, Chillingham, Alnwick, Northumberland

Dexter Cattle Society
Lomond, Seckington Lane, Newton Regis, Tamworth,
Staffs. B79 0ND

Gloucester Cattle Society
Laurel Farm, Dymock, Gloucestershire

Longhorn Cattle Society
11 Priory Terrace, Leamington Spa, Warwickshire

Northern Dairy Shorthorn Breeders' Association
9 Lennox Avenue, Richmond, Yorkshire

British Romagnola Cattle Society Ltd
7 Melville Crescent, Edinburgh EN3 7NA

Whitebred Shorthorn Association Ltd
Gap Farm, Gilsland, Carlisle, Cumberland CA1 2AY

SHEEP

National Sheep Association
Cholesbury, Nr. Tring, Herts

Black Welsh Mountain Sheep Breeders' Association
Brierley House, Summer Lane, Combe Devon, Bath
BA2 5LE

Cotswold Sheep Society Ltd
The Old Mill House, Quenington, Cirencester, Glos

Dartmoor Sheep Breeders' Association
Bilberryhill, Buckfastleigh, Devon

Herdwick Sheep Breeders' Association
Glenholm, Penrith Road, Keswick, Cumbria

Hill Radnor Flock Book Society
Newmarket Chambers, Abergavenny, Gwent

Jacob Sheep Society
Morebread Farm, Peasmarsh, Rye, Sussex

Leicester Longwool Sheep Breeders' Association
The Exchange, Driffield, East Yorkshire

Lincoln Longwool Sheep Breeders' Association
Westminster Bank Chambers, 8 Guildhall Street,
Lincoln

Llanwenog Sheep Society
Felindre-Uchaf, Cwmann, Lampeter, Dyfed

Llyn Sheep Society
Tyn Rhos, Llangybi, Pwllheli, Gwynedd

Oxford Down Sheep Breeders' Association
Boulton & Cooper Ltd, Malton, North Yorkshire

Romney Sheep Breeders' Society
Brundrett House, Tannery Lane, Ashford, Kent

Ryeland Flock Book Society Ltd
11 Blackfriars Street, Hereford HE4 9HS

Shetland Flock Book Society
Fairview, Vidlin, Shetland

Shropshire Sheep Breeders' Association
c/o John Thornborrow & Co., 11 Priory Terrace,
Leamington Spa, Warwickshire

Southdown Sheep Society
Southdown Lodge, 10 Tithe Road, Wood End,
Kempston, Beds

Teeswater Sheep Breeders' Association Ltd
Edengate, Warcop, Appleby, Westmorland

Badger-faced Welsh Mountain Sheep Society
Cwmllechwedd, Llanbister, Llandrindod, Wells, Powys

Wensleydale Longwool Sheep Breeders' Association
Bryn Goleu Farm, Cornist Lane, Flint, Clwyd

Wiltshire Horn Sheep Society
The Homestead, Kislingbury, Northants

Countrywide Livestock Ltd,
Market Place, Haltwhistle, Northumberland

PIGS

British Lop Pig Society
Trewelland, Liskeard, Cornwall

National Pig Breeders' Association
49 Clarendon Road, Watford, Herts

POULTRY

The Rare Breeds (Poultry) Society
Homestead, High Street, Congresbury, Bristol

Mrs S. Hawksworth, The Poultry Club,
Virginia Cottage, 6 Cambridge Road, Walton on
Thames, Surrey

United States

CATTLE

American Dexter Cattle Association
707 W. Water Street,
Decorah, Ia. 52101

American Pinzgauer Association
P.O. Box 1003, Norman, Ok. 73069

Belted Galloway Society
Summetville, Ohio 43962

Dutch Belted Cattle Association of America Inc
P.O. Box 358, Highlands County, Venus, Fla. 33960

Red Poll Cattle Club of America
3275 Holdrege Street, Lincoln, Nebr. 68503

Texas Longhorn Breeders Association of America
18519, 205 Alamo Plaza, Menger Hotel, San Antonio,
Texas 78205

PIGS

American Berkshire Association
601 W. Monroe Street, Springfield, Ill.62704

National Spotted Swine Record Inc.
110 Main, Bainbridge, Ind. 46105

Tamworth Swine Association
Rt.2, Box 126A, Hillsboro, Ohio 45133

SHEEP

American Shropshire Registry Association Inc
P.O. Box 1970, Monticello, Ill. 61856

American Southdown Breeders Association
Box 148, Bellefonte, Pa 16823

POULTRY

American Poultry Association
P.O. Box 70, Cushing, Oklahoma 74023

National Turkey Federation
Reston International Center, Suite 302, Reston,
Virginia 22091